Praise for *Mystically Wired*

"Smart, savvy, candid, credible, unafraid, self-effacing, and shot through with passionate love of Jesus . . . yes, hands down, this is the best book on prayer that I have ever read.

> — Phyllis Tickle
> *Compiler, The Words*
> *of Jesus: A Gospel of the*
> *Sayings of Our Lord*

"I confess, I don't normally like books on prayer, but *Mystically Wired* is a big exception. While this book is incredibly practical, I was routinely blown away by the intuitive genius of Ken's view and application of prayer. Page after page, thinking I knew what was next, I was surprised with fresh insight and unique perspectives on connecting with God. Being an evangelist, I was excited to realize I could also send this to spiritual friends who don't follow Jesus as a way to introduce him."

> — R. York Moore
> *National Evangelist*
> *InterVarsity Christian*
> *Fellowship USA*

"It began the day Jesus' disciples came to him and asked, 'Lord, teach us to pray.' Ever since, Christ-followers have been wanting to learn the ways of prayer. Ken Wilson's *Mystically Wired* is an extraordinary contribution to that learning tradition. It's a wonderful read that leaves you feeling, 'Yes, this is for me. Yes, I can do this. Yes, it's within reach.'"

> — Brian McLaren
> *Author/Speaker/Activist*

"I wandered away from religion because religion thought it had all the answers. Pastor Ken Wilson, though, understands that life and faith are really about having the right questions. If you want to pray for favors, put this book down now. If you want the answers, the help here is only partial. But if you're looking for a wide-ranging inquiry, and a path that can bring you closer to the mystery—without the mumbo-jumbo—delve within."

— Carl Safina
*Author, Song for the Blue
Ocean and The View From
Lazy Point*

"*Mystically Wired* was a breath of fresh apologetic air for me. I pray and I experience God, and I find fixed hour prayer deeply meaningful, but this book shows that God made us to do such things and our brain is wired to communicate with God."

— Scot McKnight
*Karl A. Olsson Professor in
Religious Studies
North Park University*

"In my library there are scores of books on prayer—by legends and modern guides as well. It is not easy to make a genuine contribution to this body of literature. But Ken Wilson has done so. *Mystically Wired* manages to bring together the best of the sciences and philosophies of mind, brain, and consciousness with deep spirituality and candid personal reflection. While it will happily fit my on my shelf, it fits best in a heart yearning to pray."

— Todd Hunter
Anglican Bishop

"Ken Wilson's new book is fascinating intellectually and engaging spiritually. Its theme is a great discussion starter with Christians and non-Christians alike!"

— Dr. Joel C. Hunter
Senior Pastor
Northland, A Church
Distributed

MYSTICALLY
WIRED

MYSTICALLY
WIRED

Exploring New Realms in Prayer

KEN WILSON

THOMAS NELSON
Since 1798

NASHVILLE   DALLAS   MEXICO CITY   RIO DE JANEIRO

Published in Nashville, Tennessee, by Thomas Nelson. Thomas Nelson is a registered trademark of Thomas Nelson, Inc.

Published in association with Kathryn A. Helmers, Creative Trust, Inc. Media, Entertainment & Literary Management, 5141 Virginia Way, Suite 320, Brentwood, TN 37027.

Thomas Nelson, Inc., titles may be purchased in bulk for educational, business, fund-raising, or sales promotional use. For information, please e-mail SpecialMarkets@ThomasNelson.com.

Library of Congress Cataloging-in-Publication Data

Wilson, Ken, 1952–
    Mystically wired : exploring new realms in prayer / Ken Wilson.
      p. cm.
    ISBN 978-0-8499-2001-1 (hardcover)
    1. Prayer—Christianity. 2. Mysticism. I. Title.
BV215.W49 2010
248.3'2—dc22   2009051810

Printed in the United States of America

10 11 12 13 14 WC 9 8 7 6 5 4 3 2 1

To Nancy,
who taught me what love is,
and to Dr. Sam Tickle,
whose love for the outsider
opened my heart.

By love he may be caught and held, but by thinking never.

—THE CLOUD OF UNKNOWING

My own heart let me more have pity on;
  let me be to my sad self here after, kind.

—GERARD MANLEY HOPKINS

Contents

Acknowledgments

I wish to acknowledge, first and foremost, the members of my home church, Vineyard Church of Ann Arbor, for teaching me about prayer, and for their patience with my learning curve. I am grateful for Matt Baugher, Jennifer McNeil, Stephanie Terry, and Julie Faires of Thomas Nelson, as well as Tami Heim, a woman of prayer. And for Kathy Helmers, who suggested I write this book and believed that I could. I am grateful for the influence and encouragement of Berten Waggoner, John Wimber, and many pastor colleagues in the Vineyard, A Community of Churches, who have provided a faith environment that rewards curiosity and welcomes the Spirit as a real someone.

I am indebted to Carl Safina, whose book, *Song for the Blue Ocean*, reminded me that the earth is a sacred place and that science can open the eyes of the heart as well as the mind.

My children have been a powerful inspiration for me to keep learning and questioning.

I am thankful for Don Postema, my spiritual director, and for Phyllis Tickle, who first put me on to the possibility that prayer involves going somewhere as much as doing something.

PART ONE

*Understanding That You
Are Mystically Wired*

ONE

You Are Mystically Wired

You are mystically wired. Yes, *you*. That is, you are adapted or designed to reach beyond the limits of the ingrown self to connect with the wonder of life beyond the self, including the life of God. If that sounds too good to be true, consider the possibility that it may be too good *not* to be true.

This has enormous implications for your understanding and practice of prayer. We live in a time when the landscape of prayer is shifting dramatically. Not long ago, many for whom science is the most reliable form of knowing viewed prayer as a holdover from our naïve past. The mystical modes of prayer were thought to be symptoms of mental disease. Many of history's contemplatives were retroactively diagnosed as the unfortunate if happy victims of a seizure disorder.

But that perspective is fading fast. Scientists, radiologists, and neurologists have been taking the praying brain seriously of late. These researchers have performed brain-imaging studies on monks and nuns who are engaged in meditative prayer to see if they can detect any changes in the brain that may correspond to the prayer experience.

Their findings suggest two intriguing possibilities. First, when subjects report having a particular experience in prayer, it appears that they are not simply making it up. Real shifts are taking place in their brains that convey genuine experiences of *something*.[1]

At least I'm not making this up. That was behind my relief upon reading their work a few years after undergoing a significant shift in my experience and understanding of prayer.

That is the first intriguing possibility, and the second is like it: we *all* seem to be wired for experiences that have been commonly characterized as mystical. Yes, that includes you. The praying subjects examined by the scientists were accessing portions and functions of the brain that we all have. We *all* seem to be mystically wired to some extent at least.[2]

Curious, Praying

I'm no scientist, but I'm fascinated by the research being done in this area. Neither am I a mystic, but I suspect that the prayer of the mystics is more accessible to us than we've been led to believe. This compels me to try to understand what can't be fully understood and, fool that I am, attempt to put it into words—as much for my own sake as yours.

You will find out soon enough: I'm a Jesus follower, a prayer practitioner, and a pastor (in that order). I didn't grow up with

---

1. For the most accessible description from two primary researchers, see *Why God Won't Go Away* by Andrew Newberg, MD, Eugene D'Aquili, MD, PhD, and Vince Rause (New York: Ballantine, 2002), 1–10.
2. All metaphors have their limits. They may enlighten as well as distort. "Wired" is now a common metaphor for the brain's neural network and for good reason. The brain is a network of connections that conducts impulses. Neuroelectrical signals are conveyed down the length of neurons connected with other neurons. But neurons are not copper wires, and we are not machines. And the connections within our brains are fluid, subject to change, and not static.

a strong religious orientation. "Spirit" was a category of reality that interested me only as a kind of curiosity—like the Amazing Kreskin bending forks with "psychic energy" on the *Tonight Show Starring Johnny Carson* interested me. But I'm part of a growing segment of believers who are intentionally informed by as much of the vast Christian landscape as possible: the serene liturgical part, the activist social justice part, the heartwarming evangelical part, and the "let's experience God" Pentecostal part. God is supposed to stretch our understanding, not confine it.

Belief is like a marriage partner: you fully embrace it; you learn to live with it; you also argue with it (though not usually in public); and in the arguing, if the love is working, you grow closer to your belief. I'd like to be as close as possible to mine, and I write from that place of conviction, even as I expect some of you, including those who share my beliefs, to take it all in with a grain of salt.

Matters of faith can be examined, inspected, discussed, and considered, but they can't be known from the outside. But Christianity is a "taste and see" religion, which means we *can* try it out before fully embracing it. I've tried to write *Mystically Wired* for those who like to kick the tires before taking the car for a ride.

I consider myself a slow learner in these matters. Some of my intensely spiritual friends call me "slow fizz." I suppose I've seen enough people flame out with spiritual intensity to appreciate the benefits of a slow learning curve.

Brains Itching to Pray

We tend to pray whether or not we feel we are very good at it. We tend to pray whether or not we believe that prayer is a valuable thing to do. We tend to pray whether or not we believe there is anyone out there listening. Apparently we pray because we need to, as though our brains are itching to pray.

By the time we were fit to be called *Homo sapiens*—man, the wise—we were operating with a new capacity among living creatures: to anticipate the future with an eight-cylinder imagination that went roaring into the future to scope it out and prepare for any contingencies. With that capacity came some crippling by-products: worry, fear, anxiety, and dread regarding anticipated dangers.

Prayer is what the brain does or wants to do to transcend the boundaries of the self, to sense a connection with what lies beyond the praying self.

At a very basic level, prayer is what the brain does, or wants to do, to cope with that conundrum. Prayer is perhaps one of the chief ways that we cope with an overactive fight-flight-freeze response. We pray to calm ourselves in the face of hostile opposition, real or anticipated.

Prayer is also what the brain does or wants to do to transcend the boundaries of the self, to sense a connection with what lies beyond the praying self. A certain kind of praying (and not all praying is alike) can empower our naturally self-centered selves to reach beyond the limits of our self-interest, which is ultimately in our best interest.

Praying to Get Through the Day

As one who started the discipline of daily prayer with the bogus view that prayer was a measure of holiness and therefore something I *ought* to be doing in order to be "a good Christian," I eventually learned what many praying people already know: that we pray in order to get through the day. Of course, prayer is like anything else we do to get through the day. We can do it more or less helpfully.

For years, my prayers were riddled with pious anxiety. Time to pray was often time to ruminate, to chew on the cud of my problems. When this is a staple of your praying, it can take a lot of willpower to sustain the habit of daily prayer. It took every ounce of mine. Being a full-time pastor who was, in effect, paid to be Christian, I felt an extra responsibility to keep working away at the discipline of prayer.

Through a series of unfortunate events, I ran out of energy to pray in a disciplined—that is to say a daily, intentional, and focused—way. Oh, I wanted to keep praying, but the effort required was more than I could muster.

I worked out a compromise with my praying self: I would find a prayer book, so that I could at least *say* some prayers even if I wasn't making them up from scratch; and I would explore the prayer disciplines of silence and solitude, in hopes of giving my weary brain a rest.

"Easy Does It" Prayer

Prayer with these aids was easier than prayer without them. This discovery came with a twinge of guilt. Perverse as it may sound, I felt that it was cheating. I feared that my aided prayers were somehow less authentic than my spontaneous ones. I imagined that I would soon regain my former strength and go back to a more arduous prayer style.

Instead, using these aids, I began to slip into a mode of prayer that was too lovely to dismiss. Prayer was *working for me* as never before. Prayer became more deeply restful, restorative, and strangely, creative. I no longer had to make myself pray. Instead, I looked forward to praying and schemed to do more of it.

Learning to pray can be like learning to slip out of that old party favor: the Chinese finger trap made of woven bamboo. You place your index fingers in opposing ends of the tube and push. You're in. When you try to extract them, the weave tightens. You're trapped.

Prayer became more deeply restful, restorative, and strangely, creative. I no longer had to make myself pray.

Ah, but you're smart, so you learn! Easy does it—gently push your fingers back in until the weave loosens, then gently twist as you extract them. Voila! Easy does it every time.

The brain is equipped to pray in wonderful ways, but we have to learn to gently and persistently cooperate with the way the brain works. The same applies to tapping into many of the brain's marvelous capacities. Take language, for example. Most brains come equipped with an innate capacity for sophisticated language. Nevertheless we need steady exposure to language and plenty of space to gain proficiency, which we do haltingly, bit by bit.

The ancient disciplines of prayer—the biblical disciplines of prayer—are designed to help us cooperate with the way the brain is innately equipped to pray. We gain proficiency by gentle, persistent practice.

A Shifting Landscape of Prayer

Anyone who seeks to sustain a life of prayer soon realizes that there are times when prayer scratches the itch that got you praying in the first place—and times when you wonder if praying makes any difference at all.

I had experienced blessed seasons of prayer before, but nothing like what this new "easy does it" approach, with prayer aids, facilitated. For about a year and a half I was in a kind of wonderland of prayer. It was, I suppose, a growth spurt, or perhaps a year and a half in intensive care.

Whatever it was, prayer was *different*. I noticed more wonder when my eyes were open, detecting God's winking-at-me presence in the so-called ordinary things of this world. Relationships with key people in my life were affected by what was taking place in prayer.

Prayer began to feel less like mental activity and more like going somewhere, in spite of the obvious fact that I was sitting in my usual praying spot. None of what I'd learned from the "how to pray" or "have to pray" books—the ones I stopped reading because they dulled my appetite for prayer—had prepared me for this. So I began to read a few works by or about the old Christian mystics. The language they used was remote, almost intentionally inaccessible; but for all that, it felt as though we were sampling the same manner of experience, at least in the broadest sense. This was despite my having mixed feelings about the word *mystical*.[3]

> *Prayer began to feel less like mental activity and more like going somewhere.*

---

3. Many in my own faith community are uncomfortable with the word *mystical*, largely because the word has been used to describe spiritual practices deemed to be unwise, unsafe, or unsavory. Sometimes the term *mysticism* is used to describe a set of beliefs that may or may not correspond to the Christian faith. I am using the word *mystical* in its most commonly accepted sense: as having to do with connecting with transcendent realities. A related word, *mystery*, appears many times in the New Testament, usually to refer to realities that must be revealed and are not available to our unaided senses or reason. Christianity, in this sense, is a mystical religion.

I've since realized that many people have deeply moving experiences in prayer that they rarely speak about because they simply don't have an adequate vocabulary and fear being misunderstood. These people are often not the most pious either.

The shift in my praying affected my reading of the Bible. I saw things I had never noticed before: the apostle Paul, for example was a flaming mystic whose emerging theology was rooted in divine encounters in prayer—to say nothing of Jesus or the people who wrote the Gospels, Luke and John in particular.

It's a bit like buying a new car: you see the same model everywhere you go and wonder why you never noticed that before.

Years later, I'm convinced of three things. First, it is possible to *learn* to pray in new ways; we can fall into praying ruts, but we don't have to stay there. Second, the kind of praying that was once thought to be reserved for unusually gifted (or afflicted) people called mystics is more accessible to ordinary people than previously thought. And third, the pressures of modern life, despite the modern conveniences, have heightened our need to learn and practice some of the ancient, biblical prayer disciplines.

Exploring Mystically Wired

In the first four chapters, we will explore some new ways to understand the vast landscape of prayer. Much of our difficulty praying has nothing to do with our supposed lack of effort or some intrinsic inability to pray. We lack a coherent *framework* for prayer. The thought world of the Bible is a world apart from the one we inhabit. As a result we have a great deal of trouble *making sense* of prayer, and this hinders our praying. Much of your difficulty praying, in other words, is not your fault.

In chapter 2, *You Are Mystically Challenged*, we'll explore why we feel so inept when it comes time to pray. In chapter 3, *The Year of Praying Differently*, I'll tell the story of how I stumbled into new-to-me landscapes of prayer. This will provide a foretaste of some of the prayer vistas and prayer disciplines that we will consider in more depth later in the book.

In chapter 4, *Where Do We Go When We Pray?* I'll suggest a way that we can reimagine the heavenly realms. We pray in or in relation to them but their existence as true realms can seem dubious to our modern minds. But the old story of faith and the new story of science are reassembling in some exciting ways, and it's just in the nick of time to help us pray.

In these first four chapters, don't think too much about how you might put any of this into practice. There will be time for that later. First, just consider some fresh ways of *understanding* prayer. To that end, you won't find any practical tips for prayer until the end of chapter 4.

Chapters 5 through 10, however, are loaded with things you can try to explore new realms in prayer. Keep your eye out for these prayer disciplines in particular: silence, stillness, prayer at intervals through the day, meditative practices including use of the Jesus Prayer, reflecting on scripture, and something I call "the prayer of love and remembrance."

I hope to help you appreciate how well these disciplines *fit* how our brains actually function. I think this understanding will help you practice each discipline more intelligently and motivate you to gently persist in forming some new-to-you prayer habits to enhance your praying.

These disciplines are designed to promote praying that is connected, calming, at intervals, in-depth, and eye-opening. We're mystically wired, and there's no reason not to get on with it.

You Are Mystically Challenged

"Take the next forty-five minutes to be alone with God."

I was on a short-term mission trip with my daughter and her youth group. The leaders tossed this instruction at the kids as though it were a simple thing to do, like brushing your teeth.

Time alone with God for forty-five minutes? How is that possible? It sounds *hard*. Why does it seem so hard to be alone with God? Because, in addition to being mystically wired, we're mystically challenged.

I grew up thinking that spiritual experience was something that came crashing in from another planet, another world, another order of being. Coming to faith meant becoming aware of a realm within or beyond myself that I didn't grow up recognizing—the realm of spirit, the realm of supernature to my all-too-familiar nature.

Bolstered by a few respected guides like C. S. Lewis, steeped as he was in a spirit-infused medieval mind-set,[1] I forced myself

---

1. Lewis held the Chair of Medieval and Renaissance English at Cambridge University.

to blindly trust that "spirit" was indeed a legitimate category of human experience. But alone with my thoughts, I couldn't help but wonder if I was only fooling myself.

That's part of the reason we feel mystically challenged. We think we're supposed to do our praying with something we're unsure of: our "spirit."

If I had applied the Bible's view of the human body to prayer, I might have been able to acknowledge that whatever I was experiencing, spiritual or otherwise, was happening in and mediated by my body, with a special assist from my brain. Instead, I assumed that an altogether different part of me, the spirit part, was functioning almost independent of my brain.

That's part of the reason we feel mystically challenged. We think we're supposed to do our praying with something we're unsure of: our "spirit." When we pray, it feels like our brain is doing the praying when it ought to be something other than our brain doing the praying.

Maybe we're not trying hard enough.

Too Hard to Pray?

Effort is a confusing concept when applied to prayer. Of course it takes effort to pray, inasmuch as prayer is something that happens in and with our bodies and is therefore an activity that burns calories. Prayer requires a kind of mental effort, and mental effort can be tiring. (The brain uses more energy than you might think—about 20 percent of our caloric intake fuels the brain.[2])

---

2. Arthur S. Bard, MD, and Mitchell G. Bard, PhD, *The Complete Idiot's Guide to Understanding the Brain* (New York: Alpha Books, 2002), 4.

Scientists have been puzzled for years about why we yawn, but now it seems that we yawn to cool off our brains when they have been concentrating too hard. But we don't have to cool off our brains while we are sleeping. The brain doesn't stop working while we sleep; it keeps our essential body functions functioning without any concentrated effort on our part.[3] Why can't prayer be more like that?

Though prayer does require mental effort, there are many different kinds of mental effort: concentration, attention, and intention, to name a few. It takes a different kind of effort to relax than to do math.

I used to think that connecting with God in prayer either required enormous effort or none at all. Or maybe it just took, for lack of a better word, luck. People who had spiritual experiences were the ones who were lucky enough to get zapped. How could I be more like the people who come up with three in a row at the spiritual slot machine?

If you are motivated to pray, you are probably trying plenty hard. Instead, you might need to shift the focus of your trying.

Can you imagine a way of thinking about spiritual experience that is more likely to hinder actually having one than that?

If you are motivated to pray, you are probably trying plenty hard. Instead, you might need to shift the focus of your trying. The shift might feel counterintuitive at first, especially if your intuition is to bear down harder.

---

3. Andrew Newberg, MD, and Mark Robert Waldman, *How God Changes Your Brain: Breakthrough Findings from a Leading Neuroscientist* (New York: Ballantine, 2009), 182–83.

The Kind of Effort that Doesn't Help

At the age of nineteen, I worked as a suicide prevention worker on the overnight phone hotline. I had a particularly unnerving call from a Vietnam veteran who opened the conversation by saying he had taken a lethal overdose and just wanted to tell someone why he did it. As the conversation went on, his speech became slurred until he stopped speaking entirely. There was no way to trace his location. I stayed on the line for a long time hoping that he might respond. Eventually I hung up the phone, wondering if I was the last person on earth to speak with him.[4]

I was a new Jesus follower at the time and excruciatingly frustrated over the business of prayer. I was too embarrassed to pray out loud. When I attempted to praise God, it felt like nothing in particular was happening. I so rarely felt like I was "getting through." I wanted to follow Jesus, but what did that mean if, in a bind like this, I had no clue what God was saying or doing? When that veteran called the hotline, why did he have to get me, a total neophyte?

This was not acceptable. If God was indeed around, I needed a better connection. I poured out my heart to my pastor, who invited me to stay after church and let a few young "Jesus freaks" (as they were called at the time) pray over me to "receive the Spirit." We joined forces at the altar of Messiah Lutheran Church in inner-city Detroit. After serving Communion, the pastor invited me to kneel down for the "laying on of hands" by the handful of people gathered around me.

I tried to have a spiritual experience in prayer that night. I knew *something* was supposed to happen. I didn't want to let

---

4. For a more detailed version of this story, see my book *Jesus Brand Spirituality* (Nashville: Thomas Nelson, 2008).

these well-meaning people down. I didn't want to let God down. But I didn't have a clue how to have a spiritual experience, and I wasn't even sure that such a thing was possible in my case.[5]

At a certain point, I gave up trying to have any spiritual experience at all and instead just let the people around me pray as long as they wanted to. I tried to ignore what they were doing, not to be rude but to escape the infernal mental wormhole I had entered.

I decided to occupy my thoughts by repeating the Lord's Prayer. Looking back, I think it may have been the first time I prayed the Lord's Prayer on my own since childhood. As a child I had prayed the Lord's Prayer at lightning speed every night, because I was afraid that the scary things that lurked under my bed and in the closet might come out when I fell asleep.

But I was no longer a child. I was a young father, in over his head in so many ways. In over his head being a father at an early age. In over his head working the suicide prevention phone line. And now in over his head in this business of receiving what the church called the laying on of hands.

"Our Father," I began praying silently while the others prayed over me, presumably to be blasted by the Holy Spirit.

Oddly, I wasn't able to continue beyond the opening words of the Lord's Prayer, because with those two words, uttered in a state of surrendered futility, I became aware of God's desire to be my dad. The awareness was a simple as that and as shocking as that.

New as I was to this sort of thing, I thought a spiritual experience was when the Holy Spirit made you talk in a language you didn't know or gave you the shivers or overwhelmed you with

---

5. If you've been around the Christian landscape, you may think this is turning into a book about the kind of prayer practiced in charismatic churches—what you might think of as "intense" prayer. I happen to enjoy charismatic prayer, but that's not the focus of this book.

waves of liquid love. This slightly embarrassing "God is my dad" realization wasn't on my list of approved experiences.

Only later, reading about the Spirit who makes us cry out, "Abba, Father,"[6] did I realize this might have been the real thing— an honest-to-goodness spiritual experience. And I, of all people, had had it.

Maybe prayer doesn't have to take the kind of effort we fear that it does—excruciating effort.

Whatever else it is, prayer may be the art of the humanly possible. Whatever else it is, prayer may be the art of the humanly possible. It may, of course be more than that. If God is involved, it must be more than that. But it may not be less than that.

For a person of my generation, this is a revelation, a new insight, not an assumption. I say this because I grew up on the cusp of a great shift in our understanding of spiritual experience. I grew up, that is to say, mystically challenged.

The Mystically Challenged Generation

My parents were of a generation trained to see religious orientation as an attribute of good citizenship. What we call spirituality—living a life informed and infused by spirit—wasn't on the radar of the respectably religious.

Then a wave of immigration from the East washed over us and, with it, a host of spiritualities, mainly of the Buddhist or Hindu varieties. That meant meditation—Transcendental, Zen, or

---

6. "For you did not receive a spirit that makes you a slave again to fear, but you received the Spirit of sonship. And by him we cry, 'Abba, Father.' The Spirit himself testifies with our spirit that we are God's children." (Romans 8:15–16)

otherwise.[7] This was followed by a resurgent interest in Christian spirituality, discovered anew by Pentecostals decades earlier but repackaged by their charismatic cousins for mainline consumption in the late 1960s. Baptists and Catholics, for heaven's sake, began speaking in tongues. Presbyterians began to talk about subjective experience.

My generation sat on the edge of a great transition, trying to make sense of our cravings for spiritual experience, yet lacking vocabulary for spiritual experience that didn't feel essentially foreign. Many of us ignored our cravings or pursued them privately in the realms of natural beauty or mind-altering substances; others dove into new spiritual movements, doing our best to learn the lingo, which in my case was a kind of charismatic Christianese of the biblical variety. But when you learn a vocabulary that feels like a foreign language, it leaves you wondering about the reality of the experience it describes.

Maybe this is why so many of us were simultaneously curious about and frightened of spiritual experience. In our ignorance, we assumed that it came crashing into a person like a bolt from the blue—spirit from an unknown beyond landing on spirit within that was detached or hidden away in the body, like a ghost inhabiting a house.

For a believing Christian, this assumption was grounded in a foreign theology of spirit. In biblical understanding, God as Spirit is not detached from material reality as in some other traditions. "For in him we live and move and have our being" (Acts 17:28). However transcendent God may be, he is also intimately and immediately immanent. In biblical thought, the material world is an expression of spirit, a spoken word from God. As Ludwig

---

7. Phyllis Tickle, *The Great Emergence: How Christianity Is Changing and Why* (Grand Rapids: Baker, 2008), 93–95.

Wittgenstein said, "The human body is the best picture of the human soul,"[8] a characteristically Jewish perspective.

The fact that we are material beings doesn't present an obstacle to God mixing it up with our hundred billion brain neurons[9] forming a trillion connections—this mass of tissue embedded within the rest of our body, out of which consciousness arises.[10]

God can interact with us *as we are*. He can mix it up with our fleshy, pulsating, electrically charged brains. He doesn't have to first make us into something we're not. But what did we know?

God can interact with us as we are.

The scientists who study the brain in prayer cannot shed any light on whether or not God exists. But they can remind us that if he does, and he interacts with us, it is the real us—as we are—that he interacts with.

The Question That Praying-Brain Research Legitimately Answers

People who pray and people who have mystical experiences in prayer seem to be, if anything, healthier for it.[11] It is not, as once thought, a sign of pathology. Furthermore, there is new understanding of what's happening within the brain that corresponds

---

8. Ludwig Wittgenstein, quoted in Alva Noe, *Out of Our Heads: Why You Are Not Your Brain and Other Lessons from the Biology of Consciousness* (New York: Farrar, Strauss, and Giroux, 2009), 3.

9. Like much in the realm of science, the exact number of brain neurons is in dispute; estimates range from 23 to 100 billion brain cells. Pierce J. Howard, PhD, *The Owner's Manual for the Brain* (Austin: Bard Press, 2006), 49–50.

10. For sensible understanding of human consciousness, see Alva Noe, *Out of Our Heads*, 5–7.

11. C. M. Pat Collins, *Mind & Spirit: Spirituality & Psychology in Dialogue* (New York: Columbia Press, 2006), 71–72.

to some of the benefit. Certain meditation practices, for example, can stimulate the calming mechanisms of the brain.

Does this mean that God has nothing to do with us when we meditate, that "the peace that passes understanding" (Philippians 4:7) is entirely understandable? The scientists who know the limits of their craft say, *not so fast*. In the first place, the nature of consciousness—what it is that we experience—is a complete mystery.[12] The brain is involved in consciousness, but there is no scientific explanation of consciousness. Brain scientists cannot assure us that what you experience when you see red is the same thing that I experience. There is no scientific way to "get into" or observe subjective experience. That takes a person actually having the experience. Your pain can affect me, but I cannot feel it. Is the peace people experience when they focus their mind on a rock any different than the peace they experience when they focus on the love of God? There is simply no way to tell, scientifically.

Second, scientists understand that science is limited to the study of the natural world as it is subject to the laws of nature. If the natural world is an expression of something more fundamental, if there is something that transcends the natural world, its existence could not be confirmed by the methods of science. When scientists study the brain of a person praying, they can simply note a correspondence between a reported experience and activity within the brain. The current methods of measuring neural activity don't operate at the level of fine detail: the most common neural effect that can be measured is increased blood flow to particular portions of the brain. The scientists can only say that there is increased or decreased blood flow to this or that

---

12. For a discussion of the "problem of consciousness," see Susan Blakemore, *Conversations on Consciousness: What the Best Minds Think About the Brain, Free Will, and What It Means to Be Human* (Oxford: Oxford University Press, 2006), 11–12.

portion of the brain. This is a far cry from describing—let alone explaining—what a person is experiencing.

But there is a question that we *can* answer from the scientific research on prayer: is prayer the art of the humanly possible?[13] Are we as human beings equipped, outfitted, adapted, designed, allowed, or enabled to pray—in a way that is helpful to our being and possibly the being of others?

Are we mystically wired?

I suspect that some people who keep their distance from faith do so because they see themselves as unable to engage the realm of the spirit, even if such a thing exists. Why bother with something that can't make a difference in your case? Do the deaf buy radios?

Is it possible that prayer is something we do because we are human?

Yet many more people pray than believe—and not just out of desperation. Is it possible that prayer is something we do *because* we are human? Is it possible that our brains, and not simply our beliefs, prompt us to pray?

A Case in Point: Unitive Experiences

Have you ever been about your business, and suddenly your perceptions shift and for a moment you feel more connected to people or events or everything around you as though you were but a drop in the ocean and everything around you the ocean itself?

Have you ever been sitting in a deer stand or in a boat in the middle of a lake or even in the middle of a large crowd and

---

13. By "prayer" here, I mean the activities that constitute our praying, not the actual encounter between a person and any divine realities—which must always remain a mystery.

felt strangely and wonderfully still inside? Have you ever felt, if only for a passing moment, that there wasn't such a big difference between you and the world around you?

Your brain has something that researchers Andrew Newberg and Eugene D'Aquili called the "orientation association area."[14] It's the part that allows you to experience yourself as a thing distinct from other things. This is essential so that you can navigate your way through the world without your jaw hanging open all the time.

When another part of your brain—what the same researchers call the "attention association area"—focuses intently on one thing for an extended period, the orientation association area can receive less stimulation than it otherwise would. This lessens your awareness of being separate from other things and you experience a blurring of the boundary between you and that which is not you. The researchers call this a "unitive" experience.[15]

Depending on the context, a unitive experience can feel a lot like love. Does this mean that God isn't involved when we have a unitive experience? Or does it mean that because we are made in his image, we are enabled to have such experiences? This is not a question science can answer. Only faith can.

As a person of faith, I believe the possibility of such experiences reflects the reality that we are a kind of creature able to commune consciously with God. We have come into God's world for this—to know him in this way. The psalmist exclaimed that he was "fearfully and wonderfully made" (Psalm 139:14). Our capacity to know ourselves as distinct from things around us and to have unitive experiences is part of that wonder, I believe.

---

14. Eugene D'Aquili and Andrew Newberg, *The Mystical Mind* (Minneapolis: Fortress Press, 1999), 33–34.

15. Andrew Newberg, MD, Eugene D'Aquili, MD, PhD, and Vince Rause, *Why God Won't Go Away* (New York: Ballantine, 2002), 115–17.

Prayer is more than the art of the humanly possible, but it is not less, because we are fearfully and wonderfully made. We may be mystically challenged, but our brains are mystically wired.

Perceiving Optimystically

Many of us demand too much of our spiritual experiences. We insist that an experience can only be real if it comes with the same concrete clarity of our other perceptions.

Meanwhile, prayer is one of the things we do to grope around in a landscape that doesn't lend itself to the instructions of a Global Positioning System device. Prayer is something we do when we're operating in a realm in which "we see through a glass, darkly" (1 Corinthians 13:12 kjv).

Prayer fosters a way of seeing that can help us navigate our way through the world. But this seeing is a different kind than the usual. Perhaps you've heard of a phenomenon called "blindsight."[16]

The physical act of seeing is a complex neurological phenomenon. It's not difficult to imagine that our eyes are a camera lens and our brains are the film on which the image registers. But instead, sight is a coordinated activity of many different brain centers and functions working in concert to generate the experience of seeing.

In blindsight, people who have damage to one of these brain functions may have the "lights out" experience of total blindness while their brains continue to receive visual data through the eyes, which stimulates other parts of the brain involved in seeing. When an object is placed in their field of vision, they can't "see" the object, but they can guess what it is with a much higher rate of accuracy than expected. They are able to respond to things happening

---

16. For an accessible description see "Vision Quest," *Science Illustrated*, July/August 2009, 44–49.

around them as though they have a primitive kind of sight. They can walk "blindly" while avoiding obstacles in their path as though they could see them. They may think it's just a lucky guess, but in fact their brains are processing visual data without conveying the experience we call seeing.

People with blindsight have to learn how to trust what feels like guessing but is in fact a form of sight without the normal visual experience.

Perceiving Differently

It takes a similar reorientation to learn to trust prayer as a legitimate way of perceiving. Like all learning, it can be frustrating. An infant learning to distinguish sounds goes through a great deal of trial and error before eventually decoding the rudiments of language. But infants grow into talkers.

All human consciousness is complex because it is mediated through the brain, the most complex system in the known universe. The experience of the praying brain is no different in this respect.

When we perceive God's love in prayer, there is more going on than the "raw" experience—love sent, love registered. The same is true when we perceive any love from any source. A host of factors is at play in our perception. Each factor affects the perception. If the president of the United States were to ring us up, it would probably take a while for the reality to sink in. Our first response might be something on the order of "Shut *up!*"

The Less We Trust, the Less Something Registers

Perhaps you grew up with parents who didn't know how to express feelings of affection directly. As a result, you may not trust such feelings. You may feel awkward around them, as you might feel around a stranger. As a result, the feelings of affection that you do have may not register as strongly.

Learning how to trust these emotions might require talking with someone who does. This is what keeps professional counselors in business.

A few years ago, I invited people to send me e-mails describing their experiences in prayer while I was doing a sermon series on some of the more mystical dimensions of prayer. I expected to get a few e-mails from the usual suspects—those obviously interested in such things. Instead, I received several e-mails detailing a wide range of what I could only describe as wonderful experiences in prayer from people I never suspected of having such experiences. Many of the e-mails either opened or ended with words to this effect: "I've never shared this with anyone else before, so I hope you don't think I'm crazy . . ."

We don't trust our prayer experience, not because we don't trust God, but because it involves a different manner of experience than we've been socialized to value.

People don't talk about these things because they aren't confident that they will be well received. This doesn't help us *have* such experiences. This tends to mute the experiences that we do have.

We don't trust our prayer experience, not because we don't trust God, but because it involves a different manner of experience than we've been socialized to value. To move beyond this, we may have to learn to talk about such things a little more than we do.

Language Needed

A few years ago, I began to feel something while praying that I didn't have language for. It would be more accurate to say that

I was embarrassed to use the language I had. I was having feelings of connection with the divine, but the feelings reminded me very much of the amorous feelings I have for my wife. You see my dilemma. How does an older, middle-aged man allow himself to use this kind of language for something happening in prayer?

I had a safely distant and older friend with whom I gingerly broached this topic, in the most indirect sort of way. The friend supplied me with a word, *ravishment*—as in, "Oh yes, you're referring to ravishment. This is a well-documented phenomenon in prayer and is quite normal. Haven't you read the Song of Songs?" *Good*, I thought, *this is normal*. But still, I managed to drop the subject as quickly as I possibly could. As I wish to do now.

When we have experiences that we can't even begin to put into words, we tend not to reflect on them ourselves, let alone speak of them to others. Experiences that we don't reflect on— with ourselves and with others—may be less powerful as a result. We forget them more quickly. We don't know where to file them for future reference, so they get lost.

Christianity: An Eastern Religion After All

This distrust of spiritual experience is a feature of Western civilization, shaped as it has been by rationalism, by the Protestant Reformation (which reacted against perceived abuses of spiritual experience in Roman Catholicism), and the scientific revolution. Thus, it behooves us to remember that Christianity began as an Eastern religion.

In the process of planning this book, I mentioned the title to the publisher's sales team, some very savvy and thoughtful book people. A member of the sales team wrinkled her nose and said,

"The Christian book market might not warm to a title like that. Sounds too Eastern Religion-y."

The irony wasn't lost on either of us. Christianity began as an Eastern religion.[17] It didn't begin in Oklahoma or in Western Europe. If anything, Christianity is an import from the East, not a product of the West.

> If anything, Christianity is an import from the East, not a product of the West.

But the publisher's sales rep knew that people who purchase Christian books in Christian bookstores like their religious books straight up and not served on the rocks of some other religion. Me too.

Many of the savvy readers of Christian books are aware that people who talk about meditation are often people who practice Eastern religions like Buddhism or Hinduism. They may know that Thomas Merton, a Catholic spiritual writer of the last century, learned a lot about prayer from the Zen Buddhist tradition, and this makes them nervous.

If Buddhists and Hindus meditate, then Christians don't or shouldn't—or so the thinking goes. Except that Christianity is also an Eastern religion, at least to the extent that the Middle East is Eastern. Call it an Eastern-leaning religion, if you like. Christians may meditate differently than Buddhists and Hindus—we almost certainly do in some important respects—but we all meditate. The word *meditate* is a biblical word.[18]

Despite its Eastward leanings, Christianity was adopted by

---

17. Read Philip Jenkins, *The Lost History of Christianity* (New York: HarperOne, 2008) for a fascinating history of the often-forgotten expansion of Christianity into the Eastern world.

18. See for example, Psalm 119, which uses the word *meditate* eight times.

the Roman Empire as its official religion, stamping this Middle Eastern faith as a product of Western culture. In time, Christianity as an Eastward-leaning religion went into a kind of exile. Its spirituality was overlaid with a dry-as-toast rationalism that squeezed out most of the music and the mysticism. But Christianity is now in a long process of recovering from that squeezing process. Our faith is, at long last, returning from exile.

The Need to Relax in Order to Pray

"Let's have a good conversation" isn't the best conversation starter. Too much intensity too soon, too much of the wrong effort right off the bat, doth not a good conversation make. Good conversations need a little breathing room. So does good prayer.

One of the first books I read on prayer was called *Rees Howell: Intercessor*. It was about a man who prayed with enormous intensity. He prayed day and night. He paced up and down the room in prayer. He travailed in prayer, like a woman in labor.[19]

Rees Howell: Intercessor exhausted me. I couldn't keep up with this guy. I couldn't imagine myself ever becoming the kind of person who could keep up with him. The book made me wonder if I was the praying type.

I would spare you that.

If you are wound up a little tight, begin by relaxing about your own capacity to pray. If prayer feels a little out of your depth, welcome to the club. We're all mystically challenged, because our culture has been ignoring this part of our humanity for a long time.

"My own heart," wrote Gerard Manley Hopkins, "let me

---

19. Norman Grubb, *Rees Howells: Intercessor* (Fort Washington, Pennsylvania: CLC Ministries, 1997).

*We're all
mystically
challenged,
because our
culture has been
ignoring this part
of our humanity
for a long time.*

more have pity on."[20] Have a little pity on your soul. Chances are you're not *trying* to be difficult if you find prayer to be difficult. It's just that we live in a time when many of us feel mystically challenged.

Try believing something about prayer other than "prayer is hard." Try believing that prayer isn't just for an elite few who happen to be spiritual.

Prayer is for everyone. It is the art of the humanly possible. When God is involved, it is more than that, but it is not less. Prayer is something our brains are wired to do. We just haven't been very good at teaching each other how to pray. We will get the hang of it, with a little help from our friends.

20. "My Own Heart," by Gerard Manley Hopkins, in *Hopkins Poetry and Prose* (New York: Alfred A. Knopf, 1995), 76.

THREE

The Year of Praying Differently

My father died ten years ago and gave me one last gift—a brush with depression of the grieving kind. After his death, the momentum of twenty-five years of praying ground to a halt, and I was too weary to pray in the accustomed ways, which were for me, verbally, mentally, conversationally, and charismatically.

So I allowed myself to sit still and enjoy a little quiet without having to hunt for any particular words. Meditation was on the outskirts of my prayer landscape, maybe even foreign territory. Yet I suppose I lapsed into something very like meditative prayer.

Thus began a shift in my praying that continues to this day. Please bear with me as I disclose two prayer experiences from the early years of that shift. I'm aware that unveiling personal experiences of this sort is a fraught enterprise. But it's the only way I know to move into the territory before us.

Prayer is not generic. Prayer is personal and particular. Prayer is not, and never can be, objective. Prayer is and ever will be subjective—one subject (the praying person) seeking engagement with another (God). There are experts in flying airplanes and writing computer software and baking desserts. There are no experts in prayer, because prayer involves the engagement of two personal beings, one of which transcends every category of being: God. For prayer of this sort, there are only witnesses—small voices conveying limited perspectives subject to all the human frailties that affect truth telling. With these caveats, let's dive in before we lose our nerve.

A Strange Introduction

Perhaps six months after my father died, while I was sitting in silent prayer, a surprising stillness settled over me and words formed in my mind as though not originating there, as though they were placed there by another mind: *Ken, meet Ken.* I admit to a flash of embarrassment even now as I write these words. These are words I might have dismissed as spiritual psychobabble had they not come to me in the way that they did.

I didn't disclose this experience to another soul, not even my wife, for years. I didn't know what it meant, or I couldn't put what it meant into words, or maybe I was too embarrassed by what I thought it meant, despite being profoundly grateful for the introduction. Teresa of Avila, a Spanish nun of the sixteenth century, said, "Let's not imagine that we are hollow inside."[1] Until that introduction, perhaps I had imagined that I was.

Thus began my entry into new landscapes in prayer. I slipped deeper into the practice of fixed-hour prayer (set prayers at four brief intervals through the day), which became a kind of portal into more meditative or contemplative ways of praying.

---

1. Teresa of Avila, *The Way of Perfection*, 28.10; quoted in Tessa Bielecki, *Teresa of Avila: Ecstasy and Common Sense* (Boston: Shambalah, 1996), 20.

I was getting up earlier than ever to pray, every morning without fail—a pattern I couldn't sustain before without concentrated effort. Only now, effort seemed to be the least thing this kind of praying required. At the time, I convinced myself that this wasn't a matter of discipline at all (though I'm sure the preceding years of effort exerted to pray were involved in the sense of effortlessness).

A few years later, alone in my church office early one morning, sitting in my father's worn upholstered rocking chair, something vivid and unprecedented occurred while I was praying. I had been praying the Jesus Prayer ("Lord Jesus Christ, son of the living God, have mercy on me, a sinner") for about five minutes to calm my mind for further praying, and in so doing, felt myself—excuse the metaphoric language, but what else do we have?—floating down an elevator shaft from my head to some place in the middle of my chest. It felt as close to literally like that as a thing can feel. This was something happening *in my body*.

As the sense of descent was unfolding that morning, I decided to go with it. In other words, I decided to trust that what I perceived to be happening *was* happening, even though it was beyond the borders of my expectation and previous experience.

I decided to trust that what I perceived to be happening was happening, even though it was beyond the borders of my expectation and previous experience.

That brief moment of decision was critical.

We can quench certain experiences by popping into analysis mode. It happens with emotions. Perhaps we feel something so deeply that it makes us uncomfortable. Rather than simply experiencing the emotion as it sweeps through us, we crack a joke or make a comment, because the feeling is too intense for comfort. We are muffling the feeling.

This can happen in prayer. We have to *let* certain things happen in order for them to happen. In such moments of decision—it may only take a millisecond—we say to ourselves, in effect, "This is happening and it's okay and may continue." Augustine, the North African bishop of the fourth century said, "Faith is to believe what we do not see; and the reward of this faith is to see what we believe."[2]

The aforementioned descent brought me to a visual landscape perceived with what I presume to have been "the eyes of my heart."[3] The outlines of a cave slowly emerged as if my eyes were growing accustomed to a dimly lit space. I realize, of course, that a literal cave is not located within my chest. I suppose that I realized this even as the experience was unfolding, but it didn't matter. This felt as real as anything has ever felt, even if the world was playing by a different set of rules. It felt *so* real that I'm left to wonder whether a different order of places—places as real as the ones we ordinarily inhabit—are in fact, occasionally accessible to us. Quite obviously, I'm out of my depth.[4]

A Cave, a Fire, and a Presence

Something was happening within me and yet, before my very eyes. I was aware of myself standing in the cave before a campfire with Jesus of Nazareth near me.

---

2. St. Augustine, *Sermon 43,* 1; ML 38, 254.

3. "I pray also that the eyes of your heart may be enlightened." (Ephesians 1:18)

4. For those tracking such things, the experience did not feel like a dream, or a flight of the imagination, which upon waking (or landing) feels less real. This felt as real as anything I have experienced, and this sense of "real reality" has not faded with time.

We sat together and looked into the fire, not exchanging words for a time. It was a feeling of the dearest familiarity such as I had the first time I drove in the car with Nancy when we were falling in love and we realized we were perfectly content with silence. This closeness was soon tinged with an acute sadness: I knew that in relation to the One next to me, I was a sinner. I began to cry, but not over any particular sin. It's just that I was one of those—a sinner. And I knew he knew and that he understood with me what a difficult thing it is to be: such a weight, such a hindrance, such a burden. Then I was aware of his arms around me as we beheld the fire. It was tenderness beyond description.

I asked if I could mention loved ones before him and knew that I could—and did, one after the other.

With no incentive to bring this to an end, I named as many members of my extended family as I could, then people in our church, especially members of the staff, including their family members. Which brought me to Don, whose wife, Julie, had a sister with one child, so I mentioned, "and Eileen's child." At this point the One seated next to me spoke for the first time, saying, "And another one's on the way."

A Data Point

I latched onto these words because this was a data point, linking what I knew to be a mystical experience with the world as I had always known it. I knew Don and Julie. I had met Eileen years before. Eileen was either pregnant again or she wasn't. That was my data point.

Later that day, hours after the prayer was over, I asked Don if his sister-in law Eileen was, by any chance, pregnant. "Yes, she is," he responded, surprised. "As a matter of fact, she's newly pregnant.

They're not telling people yet, as it's only a month into the pregnancy. How did you know?"

The confirmation of that data point hit me like a splash of cold water on my face. I was hyperalert and for the first time, frightened by what had happened.

I was not used to this level of intimacy. I was used to the occasional vivid sense of Jesus' presence—even, at times, an inner awareness of something he might be saying. I knew what it meant to be "led by the Spirit" (Romans 8:14). But this was different.

This closeness threatened my sense of control over my life. Jesus might at any time tell me what to do with such clarity that I'd have to just do it.

In the past, when I sensed such a prompting, I knew full well that I needed to discern whether it was God conveying a message or some other voice in my head. If there was any doubt, at least I had some wiggle room. Maybe it wasn't God after all. There was no wiggle room here, and the effect was unnerving.

As someone who has valued following Jesus for a long time, it's humbling to admit that this closeness threatened my sense of control over my life. Jesus might at any time tell me what to do with such clarity that I'd have to just do it.

That Pesky Issue of Control

There is, I think, a powerful disincentive to believe in the existence of a personal God: we might be told what to do. It's the disincentive that comes with our *attachment* to control and our unwillingness to give it up.

After years of believing in God, after years of organizing my life around such a belief, I now felt a strong disincentive to continue. Before going to bed that night, I feared that if I didn't commit then and there to praying again in the morning, I might not ever pray, at least not in that way, again.

I have a friend who had a similar experience of going somewhere when she prayed. This happened to her as a new Christian. Repeatedly she found herself sitting next to Jesus on a stone bench. She stopped going there when she prayed because a friend warned her that it sounded spooky and might be dangerous. I understand that.

Going Somewhere?

Going somewhere else—somewhere other than the usual places on our sometimes dreary mental landscape—is one of the things that move us to pray. There's something inadequate about so much of our mentation—the fact that it is so plagued by worry, for example—that we want to "go somewhere else" than wherever it is that ordinary mental awareness is happening. We're searching for other landscapes, greener pastures, and quieter waters—so we pray.

Of course, it could be that such a craving is unhealthy, that it amounts to mere escapism. But it could also be that it beckons us to enter reality more deeply. It seems that our brains are adapted, designed, or purposed to access a different interior landscape than is occupied ordinarily. It could be that we're mystically wired *for this*.

There are, in fact, two very different ways of describing the shift from *ordinary* experience to *mystical* experience. In the language of Eastern Orthodoxy, to pray is to "descend with the mind into the heart," a phrase from the contemplative Theophan the Recluse.[5] Neuroscientists describe a shift in brain activity from one portion of the brain to another when people enter a state of meditative prayer. Isn't it fascinating that both describe a shift in the "location" of prayer?

Descending with the Mind into the Heart: The Jesus Prayer

As I described, my cave experience in prayer was preceded by a sense of floating down an elevator shaft, which in turn was preceded by about five minutes of praying a simple prayer called the Jesus Prayer. It's easy: you simply pray, "Lord Jesus Christ, son of the living God, have mercy on me, a sinner" for as long as you like. We'll talk more about the Jesus Prayer in chapter 8.

The Jesus Prayer comes from the Eastern Orthodox prayer tradition. It is thought to be a way to help people "descend with the mind into the heart."[6] Nobody ever told me that either.

This language reflects the older understanding of prayer as "going somewhere." When we pray, we may enter realms we aren't usually aware of. Prayer can be understood this way: as moving from one part of the body (or the inner landscape) to another in order to connect in a different way with God, who is here but also elsewhere.

Notice carefully how the Orthodox say it: descending *with* the mind. I've heard preachers urging people to turn off your mind to experience more of God. Perhaps what they mean by

---

5. Quoted in Anthony M. Coniaris, *Introducing the Orthodox Church* (Minneapolis: Light & Life Publishing, 1982), 195–96.

6. For a brief introduction to the various uses of the Jesus Prayer, see Timothy Ware, *The Orthodox Church* (New York: Penguin, 1963), 312–14.

that is "stop overthinking things." This may be exactly what we need to do. But Paul wrote in the New Testament of the need to pray *with* the mind and the spirit (1 Corinthians 14:13–15).

"Descend *with the mind* into the heart" is a way to say, "Keep your wits about you when you pray, because you may find yourself in unfamiliar territory." The Bible forbids illicit spiritual activities, like seeking to contact the dead (Deuteronomy 18:11). Spiritual experience isn't *necessarily* good. So we are to keep our wits about us when having one. Peter spoke of the need to be clear minded, "so that you can pray" (1 Peter 4:7).

The mind, which has many different modes of activity, is but one aspect of our being. Descending with the mind into the heart is a way of saying, "Engage God from the very center of your being (the heart) as a whole person, bringing your mind with you."

The Jesus Prayer helps us to focus our minds on Jesus, ignoring the distracting cacophony of thoughts that sometimes hinder our praying, allowing us to be present to God from the very center of our being—understood rather mysteriously as a shift in location awareness within our bodies, from the mind to the heart.

> "Descend with the mind into the heart" is a way to say, "Keep your wits about you when you pray, because you may find yourself in unfamiliar territory."

Where are "you" within your body? Most of us tend to locate the self in the brain. This may go back five hundred years to philosopher René Descartes, who said, "I think, therefore I am." He was dealing with the tricky problem of how we know what we know at a time when so much assumed knowledge was shown to be wanting. Descartes, a Christian, wanted to build his philosophy on a first principle that could withstand scrutiny.

How do we know that we exist? Because here we are thinking about it and thinking requires existence. That seems like a good starting point. But can you see how that would lead us to think that our *thinking* was the center of our being? And how we came to view the self as located or centered in the mind?

This way of viewing the self—ourselves—comes so naturally to us that it sounds odd to even examine it. Yet what we call the "self" is a mystery. In biblical understanding, the self is an embodied being. The self (in Hebrew: *nephesh*, sometimes translated "soul") comes in bodily form.[7] Your "self" is in your hand or your foot as well as in your head. Better said, your body is your self because *you* are an embodied being.

When a surgeon is performing surgery with a scalpel, she doesn't simply think of her hand holding a scalpel. The scalpel is an extension of herself—she is working in and through the scalpel.[8]

Imagine extending yourself to God through an upraised open hand. You are not simply holding your hand out to God; you are presenting your self through your hand. Try it sometime, imagining that your self is located in your hand.

We can also do this with the heart. Close your eyes and imagine your self located in the center of your chest, presenting yourself to God from that location in your body. This can be conceived of as a shift in your location awareness (within your body)—from a sense of yourself focused from within your head

---

7. "Therefore . . . offer your bodies [also translated 'selves'] as living sacrifices, holy and pleasing to God." (Romans 12:1)

8. For an understanding of ways that we extend our personal presence through tools and technology, see Alva Noe, *Out of Our Heads* (New York: Farrar, Strauss, and Giroux, 2009), 82–84.

to a sense of yourself focused from within your heart, the center of the body that is you.

The Eastern Orthodox may have captured a mystery about our praying selves with their understanding of prayer as a descent with the mind into the heart.

I don't know about you, but I'm getting tired! Clearing the way for a new understanding of prayer takes a little work, but it's worth it. While I know this older way of thinking about prayer sounds strange, I think wrestling to understand it can *actually affect* the way we pray for the better.

Moving from One Part of the Brain to Another

Jill Bolte Taylor was a successful neuroanatomist when she had a stroke that completely shut down her brain's left hemisphere at the age of thirty-seven. She survived to write a fascinating memoir called *My Stroke of Insight: A Brain Scientist's Personal Journey*.[9]

Dr. Taylor's left hemisphere was completely incapacitated by the stroke. The left hemisphere of the brain is responsible for language, math, logic, and analytic thinking. It's responsible for the constant chatter you hear in your head as well as your sense of orientation in space and our experience of time as past, present, and future.[10]

With her left hemisphere silenced, Dr. Taylor experienced a very different consciousness of her right hemisphere, the center of intuition, holistic thinking (seeing the big picture and the connections between things), and nonverbal awareness. She experienced herself as fluid rather than a solid, a sense of unity with

---

9. Jill Bolte Taylor, PhD, *My Stroke of Insight* (New York: Penguin, 2006).
10. Our brains are divided into two separate hemispheres—left and right—connected by a large bundle of nerves, a kind of cable called the corpus callosum. (This connection is larger in women than men—draw your own conclusions.)

everything around her—an experience that Dr. Taylor describes as "peaceful bliss."

It was an extreme experience of moving from her "left mind" into her "right mind." This has become a more common way of talking in recent years with the growing awareness that the brain is composed of two hemispheres that perceive the world very differently, and one can learn to recognize the differences and learn to "tune in" to one side or the other.

In other words, we have a fascinating correspondence between the old way of talking about prayer as a "descent with the mind into the heart" and a new way of understanding the inner landscape, and both involve "moving from one place on the landscape to another." The old wisdom of faith and the new wisdom of science aren't necessarily in conflict. In fact if a person were in touch with the old wisdom of faith, it might provide clues for scientific inquiry.[11]

Maybe these two different ways of knowing things—faith and science—aren't incompatible, as we've been used to thinking. Maybe faith and science are actually mucking about in a reality bigger than each of them.

Better yet, maybe we're moving into a new era, when prayer can make more sense to us than it has in a long time, when we can actually begin to understand what may happen when we pray so that we can recognize it when it does and so that it may happen more frequently.

---

11. A Princeton seminary professor and a professor of physics at the New Jersey Institute of Technology made the case for the impact of older faith perspectives on the discovery of some of the breakthrough principles of the new physics, see James E. Loder and W. Jim Neidhardt, *The Knights Move: The Relational Logic of the Spirit in Theology and Science* (Colorado Springs: Helmers & Howard, 1992).

FOUR

Where Do We Go
When We Pray?

Where do we go when we pray? Anywhere we like, of course, if the question is, "Where can we do our praying from?" But I mean to ask, literally, "Where does prayer take us?" Is there a real realm that we can access, in some real sense, when we pray?

We've been reluctant to ask this question because we fear that it may not have a satisfactory answer. The story of faith,[1] as told by the Bible, suggests that when we pray, we gain access to a heavenly realm. Jesus lived, died, was raised from the dead, and ascended into heaven. When we pray, we pray "in his name" or in him. We pray in him who is in heaven.

Or do we, really?

Our sense of the real world is profoundly shaped by another story, the story of science. According to this story, heaven isn't a

---

1. I'm using the term "story" in a positive sense. Story is one of God's favorite truth-bearing vehicles, second only to persons (ultimately Jesus); and every person is and has a story. History is a story of events that are connected to one another. Our life is a story. The gospel, the message of Christianity, is the story of God in search of humanity.

real place, or so we've thought for a long time. Heaven certainly isn't a place in the way the Bible speaks of it as a place—a place "up there," just beyond the reach of the naked eye.

I would like to suggest that we lost something very important when we lost the sense that heaven is a real place. We lost something that has weakened both our understanding and our experience of prayer.

We lost something very important when we lost the sense that heaven is a real place.

In this chapter, I will consider the possibility that heaven is a real place after all, and that science, far from refuting this, can actually help us regain a sense of heaven as a real place. That's a tall order, I know. But it's important to resolve this issue if we are to feel that praying is a real thing we can do in the real world that makes real sense.

Things Need to Match Up to Make Sense

Our brains make sense of things by comparing stories. When the stories don't match up, we find it distressing.

I first got to know Phyllis Tickle by e-mail when our church asked permission to put her manual for prayer, *The Divine Hours*, online.[2] Given our common interest in prayer, we exchanged several e-mails over the course of a few years. At one point Phyllis mentioned that she and her husband, Sam, lived near Memphis when Dr. Martin Luther King Jr. was assassinated. Later, I learned that "Dr. King" occasionally visited her father and that Phyllis had fond memories of Dr. King visiting when she was a little girl.

---

2. To view this manual, see www.annarborvineyard.org/tdh/tdh.cfm.

When I first met Phyllis in person several months later, I asked her to tell me about meeting Dr. Martin Luther King. She replied, "Oh no, I never met the man. Never had the honor."

The blood drained from my head. *Who is this lady?* I thought. This new story about not meeting Dr. King didn't match up with the old story of knowing him through her father. I'd heard so many good things about Mrs. Tickle. Over e-mail, and a few phone calls, she seemed to be such a nice lady, but now her stories weren't matching up and I found it quite distressing. Was this person as trustworthy as I had supposed?

Then I did the math. Dr. Martin Luther King was five years older than Phyllis. Martin Luther King couldn't have been the "Dr. King" Phyllis met as a child in her father's study. So I asked Phyllis who that Dr. King was, and she told me it was Dr. Robert King, her family's pastor.

I had *misunderstood* the older Dr. King story. Now it fit with the newer Dr. King story, and I felt much better.

Coherence Is How the Stories Fit Together

What does this have to do with prayer? We can only make sense of prayer like we make sense of everything, by comparing different stories to see if they fit together. Most of us have been shaped by two very different stories about the world and our place in it: an older story of faith and a newer story of science. When we compare different stories, we're looking for coherence. Do the stories fit together or do they contradict each other?

We can only make sense of prayer like we make sense of everything, by comparing different stories to see if they fit together.

Coherence is part of what gives stories such explanatory power. When we see a movie with holes in the plot or credibility gaps in the acting, or errors in the inner logic of the emotions displayed, our brains judge it to be a flop. When a movie doesn't hold together, it's because the truth it is telling doesn't match up with the truth we already know. This is ultimately how we judge all our stories, including faith and science.

Something quite wonderful is now, I think, within our grasp—the barest outlines of what is to become a reassembling, a fitting back together through a growing number of connections between the older story of faith and the newer story of science. This is good news indeed, as it will help us to make better sense of prayer and this in turn, will help restore what used to be a more normal experience of prayer: prayer as place, not just an activity.

Let's begin by considering what our two most important stories—faith and science—have been telling us about prayer.

Faith Is the First Story We Hear

For most people, the older story of faith is also the first story we hear about the world and our place in it. In Sunday school, we hear Bible stories or watch VeggieTales or color pictures that tell us the love story of God in search of humanity. Someone dies and we ask where they went, and we're told "they went to heaven."

Most of us begin to pray as children when our brains are being formed by the story of faith. Robert Coles, a Harvard psychiatrist who studied the spiritual life of children actively involved in the civil rights movement, has written about the sophistication and depth of the spiritual life of children.[3]

---

3. Robert Coles, *The Spiritual Life of Children* (New York: Mariner, 1991).

I remember a very meaningful episode of prayer when I was a child. I was home sick from school in the fifth grade. My grandmother was living with us after a stay in the hospital. Things were obviously out of the ordinary that day with Grandma. My mother was occupied with Grandma and calling the doctor and my father was at work. In the middle of the confusion, I went down to the basement, knelt next to a bed there, and told God that my grandmother seemed to be suffering and that her life wasn't very enjoyable anymore, so if he wanted to, he had my permission to let her die. She died within the hour.

Children have more sophisticated prayer lives than we often acknowledge.

I have a friend who suffered unspeakable daily physical abuse as a child. She only attended church a few times with one of her aunts. But she heard a Sunday school lesson comparing prayer to "writing a letter to God every day." It was one of a very few things my friend had ever learned about prayer. It was also the last time she went to church for years. But she began to write a letter to God every day, placing the letters in a box, and burying the boxes in her backyard when they became full of letters. She credits this practice as a major factor in her psychological survival.

Faith Tells Us That We Go Somewhere When We Pray

The story of faith introduces prayer as something that involves going somewhere in, but also beyond, this world. When I speak of faith, I'm only qualified to speak of my own.

Jesus did a lot of teaching in the temple. The gospel of John especially emphasizes the temple in the ministry of Jesus. The temple was the place people went to pray, but it also represented, or *re-presented*,

The temple was understood to be the thinnest of thin spots, the place in fact, where heaven came down to earth.

the place they went to meet with God. The temple was a mystical place, in other words. It was the place where heaven and earth—two realms understood to be distinct but interconnected—intersected.

Christians sometimes infer that the temple was nothing more than a building. Not so. The Jewish people knew that the temple was meant to be what the Celts called "a thin spot." Thin spots were thought to be special places where heaven and earth intersected. The temple was understood to be the thinnest of thin spots, *the* place in fact, where heaven came down to earth.

What if there *were* such a place, an actual place where heaven came down to earth, and you could step into it, like the English schoolchildren from the Chronicles of Narnia walked into the wardrobe and came out the other side into another realm?[4]

Faith Says There Is a Place for Us

The longing evoked by Eden is the longing we have to find a place where heaven and earth intersect. This longing is the backdrop to the teaching of Jesus in the temple. It is a longing with a long history among the Jewish people—heartbreakingly evoked by the story of origins told in the second chapter of Genesis, the book of beginnings. In the Jewish imagination, the Garden of Eden was our first home on earth. It was the place where we were

---

4. The Chronicles of Narnia is a series of children's books written by C. S. Lewis in which the main characters discover a wardrobe in an empty room that leads to another world: Narnia. Children's literature is full of stories like this, including *Alice in Wonderland* and *Through the Looking Glass*.

at home with ourselves, each other, and God. This Garden was an enclosed space within the wider and wilder world described in the first chapter of Genesis. It was a place of earthly and heavenly delights. It had a river running through it—the wellspring of all life—and at the center of the garden were two trees: the tree of life and the one forbidden thing in the place, the tree of the knowledge of good and evil. Some place!

The Garden of Eden is what the temple in Jerusalem was meant to *re*-present: this place on earth where heaven and earth intersect. When Jesus stood in the temple and cried out in a loud voice, "If anyone is thirsty, let him come to me and drink. Whoever believes in me, as the Scripture has said, streams of living water will flow from within him" (John 7:37–38), he was presenting himself as the fulfillment of the temple—the place of intersection, which in due time, through death, resurrection, ascension, and the outpoured Spirit, would become available to everyone.

The rumored end to the story, told in the genre of unspeakable wonders, would bring the reintegration of heaven and earth at the time of God's choosing. In the meantime, we must pray and work and pray some more for heaven's advancing presence on earth.

Science Says Heaven Isn't Where We Thought It Was

The most troubling part of the Christian story is also the one that especially pertains to prayer: the ascension of Jesus from one place (earth) to another place (heaven). It pertains to prayer because Christians don't simply pray to Jesus in heaven; we pray in Jesus, or "in Jesus' name." That is, we pray mystically, within his person.

Where Jesus is located when prayer is happening matters, because "in his name" we go there.

Where Jesus is located when prayer is happening matters, because "in his name" we go there.

As someone who grew up in the middle of the last century, I found the ascension of Jesus to be the least believable part of my confession of faith. It seemed to be something I knew to be an actual impossibility. Jesus flew up into a place called heaven and disappeared? Yet everyone knew—and few even bothered to pretend—that heaven wasn't actually up there where Jesus went. When the astronauts circled the earth and journeyed to the moon, they weren't on the lookout for Jesus. It was space up there, not heaven.

That's a massive rupture between the story of faith and the story of science, going all the way back to the time of Galileo—the beginning of what we call the era of modern science. Galileo looked through his telescope and reported what few wanted to hear: that God and the angels were not there, contrary to what everyone believed. It's no accident of history that this was also the beginning of the end of prayer understood as "going somewhere."

Heaven Was Dislocated

This shot a hole in the Christian story heard round the world and through the ensuing centuries. Christianity is all about the kingdom of heaven breaking in to this order of things; it is about the possibility of real contact with a risen and ascended Lord, who is understood to be in heaven until the day when the two realms will be fully reunited.[5]

---

5. N. T. Wright, *Surprised by Hope: Rethinking Heaven, the Resurrection, and the Mission of the Church* (New York: HarperOne, 2008).

Heaven plays a crucial role in the story, because that's where Jesus is. Without a real Jesus being *somewhere*, there is no Christianity.

Heaven, the home of the transformed body of Jesus, began to suffer acute category confusion. For thousands of years, humans had imagined heaven as a place. All the biblical metaphors of heaven—the realm beyond this one where God dwells in fullness—are place metaphors. Virtually overnight, the image of heaven as a place was shattered.

We faced a choice: either drop the idea of heaven altogether, or attempt to reimagine heaven as something other than a place (and the kingdom of heaven as something other than a realm). As heaven became an unreal place, our faith began to feel to us like an unreal thing. We might continue to practice it, but deep inside, we feared that we were just pretending.

This is the confusion I grew up with in the middle of the last century. The influential thinkers of the time opted to view heaven as an idea, not a place—an idea whose time had come and gone. Which meant traditional religion was an idea whose time had come and gone. It was an idea to grow out of, not into.

I was the youngest of three children. I watched my older sister outgrow our Episcopal Christian faith in high school. So when I read *The Fountainhead* by Ayn Rand in junior high school, it gave me what I needed—a more credible account of reality to grow into, as I grew out of my faith like an old pair of tennis shoes.[6]

How did Christians carry on in light of heaven's dislocation? They imagined heaven as something decidedly other than

6. Ayn Rand, *The Fountainhead* (New York: Signet, 1996). This novel ends with the protagonist making a glorious ascent in a skyscraper built as a monument to the autonomous human. The ending appealed to my adolescent sensibility, and I jumped up in my bed at the novel's end, thrusting my upraised fist into the air before no one in particular.

a place. Heaven wasn't a place, and there weren't people floating around playing harps on clouds up there. I can hardly remember a serious discussion of heaven that didn't begin with this caveat, made ponderously clear.

We were told that heaven was a "state of being" like a state of mind. But even a state of mind is somewhere—in a brain of flesh and blood, for example. Where was Jesus in his risen body, if not somewhere? We were left to believe that Jesus was physically raised from the dead but no longer present in any particular place.

If heaven is not a place, then it is not a place for beings like us. That seemed to be the takeaway.

Science Had Second Thoughts about Three-Dimensional Places

The physics I learned in school was the old physics of Sir Isaac Newton, which depicted the universe as a closed system ruled by cause and effect. If one could only know all the laws of physics in such a closed system and all the conditions within the system at any given time, it would be possible, given enough computational power, to predict exactly what would happen next. (Stick with me; this all applies to prayer!)

Fortunately, the story of science was going through a radical revision, a shakeup prompted by the new physics of Albert Einstein. Perhaps we don't exist in three-dimensional space as we once understood three-dimensional space. Perhaps the three dimensions of space are integrated with another dimension, time. Einstein's theory of special relativity revealed a world in which space and time were joined dimensions, with time bending, speeding up, and slowing down according to local conditions.

The new physics revealed a universe in which subatomic particles—which weren't particles at all but something more like mathematical probabilities—popped into and out of existence. Yes, into and out of existence. The more the new physics revealed about matter, the less matter looked like the thing we thought it was: predictable, substantial, inert, solid stuff.

The principle that blew the cork out of the bottle of the new wine of the new physics, the wine that made us all feel a little loopy, was aptly named Heisenberg's Uncertainty Principle. This principle holds that it is impossible to know both

Perhaps the three dimensions of space are integrated with another dimension, time.

the location and the momentum of an entity like an electron, one of those subatomic particles that is not really a particle. It's not just that we don't have the equipment to measure this. It's that it can't be known, because it is inherently unpredictable. As John Gribbin says, "The electron itself can't know where it is and where it is going."[7] Until this time, science had the hope of attaining certainty about a certain world, even if it might never be realized. Now science was embracing the certainty of uncertainty, the probability of certain unpredictability—at the very heart of things. I know, it's enough to turn your head inside out!

The closed universe of classical physics was at best a rough approximation that broke down at the scale of the microquanta.[8] If the position and movements of the smallest expressions of matter and energy could not be predicted—because they are inherently unpredictable—how could the system not be open?

God could easily influence whatever he wanted to at the quantum level with no possibility of us either detecting such influence

---

7. John Gribbin, *Get a Grip on New Physics* (London: Weidenfeld & Nicolson, 1999), 102.

8. Scientists understand *quanta* as the smallest possible form of energy or matter.

or ruling it out. (Since our brain is affected by action at this level, God's influence there is equally imaginable.)

As experiments revealed smaller and stranger subatomic particles with names like "quarks" and "bosons" and "muons," physicists began to theorize that at the smallest level of matter, there may be multiple dimensions beyond the four dimensions of space time.[9]

You see where I'm headed. The concept of place, a function of the universe that we once thought to be simple and understandable (if vast), is much stranger, much more mysterious than anyone thought. Unbelievably weird would be an apt description. Scientists, not just science-fiction writers, now speak with a straight face of parallel dimensions and a multiverse—of which our known universe is simply one.

Not much of this revised telling of the story of science made its way into my public school science classes. We learned the old science, which still applied, of course, but it wasn't the whole story. Gradually, the new science began to leak into the popular culture, which in my generation was driven by television.

The new physics first appeared in *The Twilight Zone* with Rod Serling. Then came *Star Trek* and its successor *Star Trek: The Next Generation*, futuristic dramas about space travel at high speeds, which meant the theoretical possibility of time travel as well, according to the new science. Oh, and wormholes providing shortcuts between vast distances within the universe, or maybe access to parallel universes or hitherto inaccessible realms within our own universe, and black holes that offered to lead us all into Alice's Wonderland.[10]

---

9. See Brian Greene, *The Elegant Universe: Superstrings, Hidden Dimensions, and the Quest for the Ultimate Theory* (New York: Vintage, 2000), if you have the nerve.

10. For a historical overview, see Lawrence M. Krauss, *Hiding in the Mirror: The Quest for Alternate Realities, from Plato to String Theory (by way of Alice in Wonderland, Einstein, and The Twilight Zone)* (New York: Penguin, 2005).

For the first time in a long, long time, for those who were paying attention, the story of science began to connect again with the story of old-time religion, like a nerve ending finding its way to a neighboring neuron and beginning to fire, to connect, to form a new pathway.

Maybe Heaven Is a Place After All

What if all the embarrassed protesting that heaven isn't a place was premature?

What if heaven can be understood as a place, albeit a different kind of place? What if heaven is analogous to one of those extra dimensions or parallel universes that can only be inferred mathematically?[11] If parallel dimensions could be inferred with math, couldn't heaven be inferred with faith?

Could heaven be imagined as a dimension or set of dimensions running alongside or even within but also beyond the space-time four? Could we imagine heaven as the dimension or set of dimensions out of which space-time exploded in the big bang, to use that language? Now, in a very real sense, in a potentially actual sense, we're getting somewhere. When we pray, that is.

For those who pray to a God who dwells in a realm called heaven, the location of heaven is not a moot point. It pertains to the reality of the praying experience.

When I pray to a God who dwells in heaven, is it possible that I'm doing something other than exercising my religious imagination? Is this real or fake?

For the first time in a long time, those who confess a crucified, buried, risen, and ascended-into-heaven Lord have a

---

11. I'm not suggesting that heaven is such a place, simply that it is analogous to, or like, such a place.

way of imagining heaven as a place—where *he* is—that doesn't require choosing between the story of faith and the story of science. The two stories might be complementary. For the believer, this opens up the possibility that in believing, we aren't simply kidding the part of ourselves that believes the story of science.

When I pray to a God who dwells in heaven, is it possible that I'm doing something other than exercising my religious imagination? Is this real or fake?

Heaven as a transcendent dimension—analogous to a third dimension in a two-dimensional flatland, infinitely near yet infinitely beyond the two dimensional flatland[12]—fits the experience that the earliest Jesus communities had of their ascended Lord. After his ascension, these communities experienced Jesus as nearby, not far away. Surely prayer was part of this experienced proximity. When Mary met the risen Lord in the garden, she was told not to cling to him because he wasn't yet ascended, implying that once he was, they could be nearer (John 20:16–17). For the first time in a long time, we can imagine the possibility that when we pray, we may in fact be going somewhere.

The Internet Is Another Point of Intersection

Prayer happens in, or at least with, our brains. This network of a trillion neural connections manifests an ever-shifting, cascading, arranging and rearranging sequence of electrical storms conveyed

---

12. See Edwin Abbot, *Flatland: A Romance of Many Dimensions* (New York: Penguin Classic, 1998), the fanciful story of geometric-shaped figures seeking to make sense of a recently discovered third dimension.

by neurochemical transmitters. V. S. Ramachandran writes, "It has been estimated that the number of possible permutations and combinations of brain activity, in other words, the number of brain states, exceeds the number of elementary particles in the known universe."[13] Networks are capable of phenomena far beyond our capacity to grasp.

Our brains are aided by another network that they have helped to generate: the Internet, a network of computer servers linked to each other around the world, which are in turn linked to hundreds of millions, perhaps by now, billions of computers. This network, invented by humans, has a suprahuman quality.

The Internet is not controlled by any human institution or organization. It is a global network that crosses virtually every tribal, national, and geographic boundary. It is an invention that even its inventors have difficulty grasping. Like a city, it has a life of its own, likely to outlast our own. And like a city, for those who dwell therein, it is a part of our everyday experience. It is part of the story that informs our everyday lives.

The Internet is a form of reality that we call *virtual* in an attempt to say that it runs parallel to the ordinary reality of life in the world.

We refer to this network as a place. We *go online* through a portal, our computer or cell phone loaded with software. There we do our business and then go offline.[14] In much the same way that we pray.

Prayer is a way for us to access the network of Spirit—the kingdom of heaven—spun forth from the God of love. We enter through a portal, our mystically wired self, descending with our minds into our hearts, through which we pray "in Jesus' name"

---

13. V. S. Ramachandran, *A Brief Tour of Consciousness* (New York: PI Press, 2004), 3.
14. Phyllis Tickle, *God-Talk in America* (New York: Crossroad, 1998), 143–45.

and commune with him where he is—what the apostle Paul called "the heavenly realms" (Ephesians 1:3, 20; 2:6; 3:10; 6:12).

Our hearts are equipped for this connection by the gospel story, a software package updated by our ongoing experience of grace. This "connecting software" shapes where we go when we pray and how we get there.

Let's flesh this out a little more. What if the kingdom of heaven is something like a network of persons, a network whose nodal points are persons?[15] The nodal points are linked by love—relationship between persons. When the network is infused by the presence of God, the links between persons are lit up by love in the way that a computer network or the network of nerves that constitutes a brain is lit up by electrical impulses.

The network is always there, and in some sense we are always on it. We couldn't exist apart from God's sustaining presence.

Prayer is one of the ways we become more consciously aware of the vast network that is an expanding manifestation of the love within and between the Trinity: Father, Son, Holy Spirit. Prayer is one of the primary ways we have of "improving our conscious contact with God," to use the phrase in the eleventh step of Alcoholics Anonymous.[16]

Could We Dispense with the Metaphors and Talk Straight?

We talk straight by use of metaphors. We can only understand anything by way of correspondence with other things. The problem is we don't have enough metaphors to shine a light on prayer.

---

15. A nodal is a junction point in a transmission system.
16. Step 11: Sought through prayer and meditation to improve our conscious contact with God as we understood Him, praying only for knowledge of His will for us and the power to carry that out.

The most common metaphor for prayer is conversation—prayer is like having a conversation with God. It's a very helpful metaphor, but like all metaphors, it both highlights and hides aspects of prayer.[17]

Prayer is like a conversation with God in *some* respects, but not others. We can speak words to God, and God hears our words. But this metaphor also hides the reality that while we share God's image, we differ from God in important ways, and this affects prayer: we are flesh and blood, and God is spirit. Hearing from God is different than hearing from other people. Too often, we glibly toss out the conversation metaphor as if that's all we need to know about prayer, and it leaves people frustrated.

I've introduced some new metaphors to highlight the context for prayer that we find in the Bible and in the experience of pre-modern prayers: prayer as a place.[18] Your head may be spinning with the introduction of these new metaphors: parallel dimensions, the Internet, networks with nodal points—give me a break!

But there's a point to all this that's worth all the work. To pray is not simply to converse with God. To pray is also to go somewhere in order to commune with God. The place metaphors are not meant to replace other useful metaphors, but to supplement them.

The plain fact is we can't talk about the kingdom of God without using metaphors, because the kingdom of God is a reality far beyond our mortal reckoning. Jesus referred to "the mystery of the kingdom of God" (Mark 4:10 NKJV). He used

---

17. George Lakoff and Mark Johnson, *Metaphors We Live By* (Chicago: The University of Chicago Press, 1980), 10–13.

18. The Catholic mystic Theresa of Avila used this metaphor in her classic work on prayer titled *The Interior Castle*; it is also a favorite metaphor for prayer in the writing of Phyllis Tickle, see especially *The Shaping of a Life: A Spiritual Landscape* (New York: Image, 2003), and *Prayer Is a Place: America's Religious Landscape Observed* (New York: Doubleday, 2005).

one metaphor after the other, drawn from the everyday life of his hearers to reveal the kingdom: the kingdom of God is like a net, a pearl, a treasure hidden in a field, a sower going out to sow, a mustard seed, and so on.

New metaphors take time to work out and time to sink in. We ponder the possible correspondence first, just as the disciples did with Jesus' parables of the kingdom—often returning to ask Jesus to draw out the correspondence more explicitly.[19] This process is part of seeking the kingdom of God.

There Is a Continuum
of "Place Experiences" in Prayer

There is no "normal" experience of prayer. As Don Postema, my spiritual director, once told me, "Prayer is as personal as your toothbrush."[20] Normal is not a very helpful concept when applied to prayer, especially the interior experience of praying.

There is no "normal" experience of prayer.

Not all prayer involves some form of altered awareness. Dramatic or vivid things may happen, and ordinary or subtle things may happen.

This extraordinary capacity of our brains to go somewhere can feel very ordinary. When we anticipate the future by imagining it, we are visiting potential scenarios. When we remember something, we are revisiting the past. When we listen to music, watch movies, or read stories, we may be going "somewhere else" with our brains.

---

19. "When he was alone, the Twelve and the others around him asked him about the parables." (Mark 4:10)
20. I highly recommend Don's book, *Making Space for God: The Study and Practice of Prayer and Spirituality* (Grand Rapids: Faith Alive Christian Resources, 1997).

We settle into prayer and we toss prayers off the top of our heads. Like the other day, when I saw the police officer walking to my car after pulling me over for speeding. "Lord, please make it a warning, not a ticket!" I prayed.

I got the warning that time. The previous time, I got the ticket. Maybe I should slow down.

There is not some invisible mystical threshold to cross. All experience, including prayer, happens along a continuum.

Have you ever prayed with a group of people in a living room? Perhaps something about the people or the setting made you feel especially at ease and the prayers of the group connected. As one person after the other spoke simple words of prayer aloud in the group, you could feel an invisible bond holding the group together. The atmosphere shifted subtly but perceptibly—*thicker* might describe it.

Together, you had gone somewhere: "closer to God" or "into his presence." It may take a little extra attention to notice this, but there *is* something to notice.

So it's not that this is such a strange phenomenon. It's just that we haven't thought of prayer as "going somewhere" in a long time.

Why Was That Such Hard Work?

The process we just went through was mentally demanding, not because prayer itself requires brain-busting work, but because the task of reimagining prayer in the twenty-first century requires it. We are recovering something that has been lost. We are in a time when a new language for prayer is being developed, one that integrates major stories of ancient faith, modern science, and everyday experience by finding connections between them all.

In the early part of the twentieth century, Eliezer Ben-Yehuda led an amazing process that resulted in revival of Hebrew as a modern language. Hebrew at that time was considered a dead language, used only by scholars dealing with ancient documents speaking the language of an ancient culture. Eliezer Ben-Yehuda, helped by a group of idealistic graduate students, recreated Hebrew as a language for use in the modern world. Being a reassembled language, Modern Hebrew required a community of people motivated to learn it and use it. One imagines that it was awkward at first, and that as the community increased, the language was developed.

Something like this is needed for prayer—a new language, partly revived and partly invented anew, and a new community to give meaning to the words by the power of shared experience.

In the Meantime, Make a Praying Place

Perhaps you've noticed that I haven't made any practical recommendations about how you might improve your experience of prayer yet. That's because I think a great deal of our difficulty praying has to do with how we understand what prayer actually is. We have to dig deeper down into our understanding of prayer and spiritual experiences before the practical advice gets us anywhere.

A great deal of our difficulty praying has to do with how we understand what prayer actually is.

But now, having been put through the paces, you're ready, I think, for a little practical advice.

Do you have a place to pray? That is, do you have a designated place in your everyday living space, that is specially set apart for prayer? If not, get thee one. You may have the luxury of setting aside an entire room in your house or apartment for prayer. More likely, you'll be able to designate a place in a room—a comfortable chair with an end table and lamp, say, as your praying place.

My praying place is in my home office. It's in the corner near the window, with a bird feeder attached by suction cups to the outside pane. I have a comfy chair and one of the end tables from home growing up. I'm careful what I put on that end table: a favorite icon representation of Jesus ("not made with human hands"—a Russian Orthodox icon), a bamboo plant growing in a vase of water (no feeding or tending required—just my botanical speed), and a cool thing my kids gave me for Father's Day, an orb of enclosed water with a few brine shrimp swimming around. Is that more information than you wanted?

I can close the door to my office. I can dim the lights. I can light a candle in there. I can connect my laptop to some speakers and listen to some music if I'm in the mood. Does ten or fifteen minutes sound too long to bear? Try three minutes at first.

I try not to use my praying space for anything onerous, like paying bills or having a difficult conversation with someone. I've set it up to make it a place I enjoy going to. I get a good feeling just sitting there, and all the more after my wife painted the office a dark red-brown with a texture effect that makes it look like leather. A womb with a view, I call it.

Prayer happens in and with our bodies, so it helps us to have a physical place that we want to inhabit while we pray.

Practice the Be-in-a-Room Exercise

The French mathematician philosopher Blaise Pascal said, "All of man's troubles stem from his inability to sit quietly alone in a room."[21] Learning to sit quietly alone in a room makes a big difference in your praying.[22]

Anthony Bloom, a physician, member of the French Resistance during World War II, and archbishop in the Eastern Orthodox Church—advised a woman who was having difficulty praying to simply find a nice spot in her home and take some of her knitting and sit quietly in the room, soaking in her surroundings. It helped the woman to relax, which helped her to pray.[23]

Once you've made your praying place, try it out. Just take ten or fifteen minutes to sit there quietly. Pascal didn't say how long a person had to sit alone in a room. Try to notice the room, focusing on the things you like about the place. Notice the chair—how comfortable it is. Look out the window. Compared to say, being stuck in traffic in the sweltering heat with no AC, isn't it a nice place to sit? Keep your eyes open to take in the view; focus on what you enjoy about the room; perhaps close your eyes to listen to the sounds surrounding you. Just enjoy the placeness of the place.[24]

---

21. Blaise Pascal, *Pensées* (New York: Penguin Classics, 1995).

22. That's not to say sitting alone in a room is the only way to pray. Lots of people find that walking better enables them to pray. More on that in chapter 9.

23. Anthony Bloom, *Beginning to Pray* (New York: Paulist Press, 1970), 92–93.

24. To take this prayer exercise one step further, once you have acclimated to the place as described above, read Ephesians 1:3–10 and try to imagine a place that was characterized by the words Paul used to described the heavenly realms.

PART 2

*Exploring New Realms
in Prayer*

FIVE

Connected: The Prayer of Love and Remembrance

We are never alone when we pray, and I just don't mean alone from God. We are never alone from a surrounding community, even when there isn't a soul in sight.

One New Testament author wrote that "we are surrounded by a great cloud of witnesses" (Hebrews 12:1), referring to men and women who have died, yet live before God. He doesn't argue the point: he is simply reminding the community of something they already know. They are surrounded in the present by those who have preceded them in the way of faith.

How would our prayer be affected if this were our shared understanding, something so well known that it could simply be referenced without explanation? We would feel less alone and more connected.

We are never alone when we pray.

And we would feel more buoyed. "Since we are surrounded by such a great cloud of witnesses, let us throw off everything that hinders and the sin that so easily entangles, and let us run with perseverance the race marked out for us" (Hebrews 12:1).

When I ran the mile on the high school track team, we had bleachers on one side of the oval track. My dad and my girlfriend, Nancy, came to most meets. We all ran faster when we ran past the stands. You couldn't help it. On the opposite side of the track you felt alone, but in front of the stands you felt buoyed, because you were.

The first "not good" in the Bible had nothing to do with the subsequent fall from grace. "It is not good for the human to be alone," said God in the garden before anything had gone wrong (Genesis 2:18 ALTER).

People who enjoy praying in solitude often do so because in solitude *they don't feel alone*. The noise of the crowd subsides, and they are aware of themselves surrounded by the cloud of witnesses.

The more we become aware that a cloud of witnesses surrounds us, the less we dread being alone to pray.[1]

It Feels Good to Be with People Who Feel Good

You can feel a person's presence without seeing him or hearing him or touching him. If someone is in the room, you may simply sense that he is present. No doubt we're adapted or designed to notice the presence of others like that, if for no other reason than that it enhances our chances of survival.

On Sunday mornings before church, I get up extra early to pray. It's dark and quiet. I light a candle and say my morning

---

1. As a Christian, of course, I also believe that the grace extended to me in the beloved Son removes the shame of my sinful condition, which otherwise hinders me from standing before God with a clear conscience.

prayers to begin. One Sunday morning, something unusual happened. As I was sitting in silence, I felt my father sitting next to me on the sofa. This was about five years after he died.

I mean, of course, that I felt the presence of my father sitting next to me—to my right, in fact. I dared not open my eyes to look, because I knew I would just see the sofa and no father.

I've no idea how long the sense of his presence lasted. I didn't have the slightest inclination to say anything to or to hear anything from my father. The sense of his presence was enough, especially as I knew that he was well. It was well with his soul.

That was probably the purpose of the sense of nearby presence that morning—reassurance.

I've no idea what it is, but there is something in a son, sometimes, that doesn't feel right about being taller or faster or smarter or more successful than his father; or happier, as I felt happier than my father, who lived with more than his share of unhappiness. Knowing of his unhappiness through so much of his life was a cloud over my happiness, and that morning, it seemed as though the cloud lifted. It came as a welcome relief.

It Feels Good to Feel Connected

Lesslie Newbigin, British missionary and theologian, says that cultural worldviews and their respective religions come in three basic forms: atomic (highlighting the individual unit), oceanic (all things merged into one), or relational. Christianity, he said, is relational to the core.[2]

The first self-reference—God referring to himself—in the Bible is not the word *I* or *me* but the word *us*. "And God said, 'Let

---

2. Lesslie Newbigin, *The Gospel in a Pluralist Society* (Grand Rapids: Eerdmans, 1989), 171–72.

us make a human in our image, by our likeness'" (Genesis 1:26 ALTER). This, in the founding book whose primary revelation is that God is One: "Hear, O Israel: The Lord our God . . . is One!" (Deuteronomy 6:4).

This is the mystery of the Trinitarian understanding of God's oneness: he knows himself as an "Us"—a community of persons, Father, Son, and Holy Spirit. God is, within himself, irreducible relationship. Or to say it another way, God is love: the Father who is ever-generating Love, the Son who is ever-receiving Love, and the Spirit who is ever-consuming or burning Love. Out of this generating, receiving, and consuming love, all that is and ever will be "flames out," as the poet G. M. Hopkins says, "like shook foil."[3]

God is a connected and connecting Being. When we are brought into relationship with God through Jesus, we are, as Jesus said, grafted into a vine as branches are—an early network metaphor to describe the kingdom of heaven (John 15:1–17).

Try this sometime: imagine the spiritual realm that is our home in Jesus—the kingdom of heaven—as a network like the brain is a network of neurons. The kingdom of heaven has always been a network of never-ending, ever-beginning, ever-generating love—Father, Son, and Holy Spirit—expanding to include anyone who will not reject this love.

Have you ever seen a graphic depiction of a network? A fishing net is a simple example in two dimensions. Go online for an image of a neural network, brain neurons linked to each other in three dimensions. There are some nice ones in which the connections between neurons look like points of light linked to each other in a network.

---

3. Gerard Manley Hopkins, "God's Grandeur," *Hopkins: Poems and Prose*, Everyman's Library Pocket Poets (New York: Alfred A. Knopf, 1995), 14.

Imagine yourself in this kind of arrangement with those who are on the network with you. Those whom you know and love are directly connected to you.

You are small, not big. You are not the center of anything, but you are surrounded. You are connected. The God who is love flows through the connections, and so you are in touch, directly or indirectly, with all of it, wherever you may be on the network.

The context of all prayer is love of the networked kind.

What you are imagining when you do this is not so much prayer itself, as the context of all prayer. The context of all prayer is love of the networked kind.

Your Brain Wants to Be Pickled in Love

I wonder if "design" is the most serviceable metaphor for God's creative power.[4] I wonder, instead, if God imagines things, and part of his imagining things is imagining that they are also free in some sense to become what they will be, so that God can have the joy of letting some things show themselves to him.[5] This way of creating is more relational than mechanical. In a world like this, love, not power, would be the strongest bond.

To be in touch with such a reality then, would be to be pickled in love—completely soaked in love so that we wouldn't spoil with time.

The mystically wired brain is meant to imagine a reality leaning in this direction, and to feel, perceive, sense, and experience such a thing as this. The word *mystical* means many things to many

---

4. I owe this insight to Bill Elkington, who blogs at www.mysticbelieverpriest .wordpress.com.

5. I'm indebted to Dr. Jorella Andrews, senior lecturer, Goldsmiths, University of London, for this notion of things "showing off."

people, but *this* is what it means to me to say that we are "mystically wired": our brains are meant to catch a whiff of this reality. Our brains are wired to be pickled in love.

I stumbled into this way of praying on vacation several years back. Being the sort of person who has gone to the same place for vacation for the past thirty years, I find certain routines relaxing. One of them is an hour-long walk to nowhere in particular and back.

What do you do with your brain while walking, especially if you're of a generation that doesn't wear earbuds? You look around and you think. But this can become less than relaxing as you think about work, for example, or the economy.

So your brain, seeking relief from this, looks for something else to think about. And thus by a process of elimination as much as inspiration, the brain agrees to pray. But what do you pray about? Problems? More work. How about people?

We all know that we can pray for people, even dear loved ones, in a problem-solving way. The analytical portion of the left hemisphere, the one that gets trained and fed by years of schooling, is quite adept at this: scanning the horizon in search of gaps or missing pieces or problems that need attention. It's how we get things done.

Except that it's not how we get rest done, and this was my goal on vacation, to rest myself, including my brain.

So I made a deal with my brain for that vacation's praying: no praying for people as I walked, except people I loved and I knew loved me, and no problem-solving prayer for such people. That is, no focus on any of their faults, weaknesses, or deficiencies, even with the best of intentions—that they be given enormous help from God to overcome said faults, weaknesses, or deficiencies.

What I experienced over that vacation's walking prayer, an hour a day every day, was nothing short of delicious. It turns out that I love several people, and I know without a doubt that several people love me. I held them, one at a time, in memory for brief or extended portions of my walk each day, focused as much as my brain allowed on the simple fact that I loved each one and knew each one loved me. This induced an unexpected result: I felt myself to be pickled in love.

You really should try this sometime.

Is This What Paul Meant?

The next time I read Paul's letter to the Ephesians, I couldn't help but wonder if his experience praying had any correspondence to mine: "For this reason, ever since I heard about your faith in the Lord Jesus and your love for all the saints, I have not stopped giving thanks for you, remembering you in my prayers" (1:15–16).

I find Paul to be a compelling witness on so many things. Paul can come across as self-absorbed, concerned about his reputation, or upset by a slight or an insult. There's someone I can identify with!

My father found reading Paul's letters difficult.[6] I came to faith before my father had reactivated his own, so I gave him a Bible to read. One afternoon while visiting my father at his house, he came fuming out of the dining room where he had been reading his new Bible, saying, "This Paul! What an arrogant egomaniac! Who let him write the Bible?" My dad was reading Paul's second letter to the Corinthians.

---

6. My father was in good company: the apostle Peter wrote, "His [Paul's] letters contain some things that are hard to understand" (2 Peter 3:16).

Lots of people find Paul difficult. Peter might have found him difficult to get along with, as did other leaders in the early church, like Mark, the cousin of Barnabas.

To me, this doesn't hinder Paul's witness. It enhances his witness. When the irascible Paul spoke of love in such over-the-top terms, I wanted to sit up and take notice. Perhaps I, too, could experience love if he could.

As I read the context of Paul's words about his prayer of remembrance of those who love him, I see a man who had gone a little tipsy over God as he came to know God through Jesus of Nazareth.

Before coming to faith in Jesus, I smoked what was then a pretty mild form of marijuana. One of my first acts as a new follower was to flush the last of my marijuana stash down the toilet. Somehow I knew that getting high wasn't the Jesus-following thing to do.

Under the influence of marijuana, I had this mellow, everything-is-okay-and-everyone-loves-everyone-else feeling. Sometimes. Other times, I just felt bored, depressed, empty, and mellow. But even when the lovely feeling arrived, it was extremely disappointing because it left when the high faded.

Paul seemed to have known a sober-minded sense of mystical love, which he wrote of in the first chapter of his letter to the Ephesians. You can hardly keep track of what he was saying, because he gushed about love and heavenly realms and Christ Jesus and blessing and pleasure and glory and praise and forgiveness and riches of grace and mysteries and of all things coming together. I don't think a guy like Paul writes like this unless he's experienced something out of which he writes, something that makes me hungry for what it is he's bearing witness to.

Understand the Power of Memory
in Prayer and Love

Paul was referring to the power of memory as a conveyor of love. "For this reason, ever since I heard about your faith in the Lord Jesus and your love for all the saints, I have not stopped giving thanks for you, remembering you in my prayers" (Ephesians 1:15–16).

Most of our experience of love happens in memory. In fact, without memory, love isn't possible—or it is something very different than love with memory. This is the tragedy of having a loved one who suffers from advanced Alzheimer's disease—to be forgotten by a person who has loved you all your life. Despite what the gurus tell us, simply "loving in the now" isn't what it's cracked up to be.

Love happens in memory because we don't relate to people only when we are in their physical or digitally conveyed presence. We also relate to the presence of the person stored within us in the form of memory. And the way we relate to their presence stored in memory has a big impact on the way we relate to them in real time.[7]

Most of our experience of love happens in memory.

As it turns out, the Jewish people had a vivid and powerful understanding of memory. There are various versions of "Remember us!" prayers in the Bible.[8] Were they afraid that God had forgotten them, owing to a poor memory?

---

7. To be a little more precise: even when we relate to a person who is standing in front of us, it is our consciousness of the person mediated through our brains that we are interacting with. From this perspective, the memory of the person is not so far removed from our other experience of him.

8. See, for example, Psalm 74:2.

No, they had what might be called a higher view of memory. To be remembered isn't simply to register on someone's mental landscape. To be remembered is to be *held in memory*. The word itself in English suggests something powerful: to be *re*-membered.

Recall *Star Trek*'s famous phrase "Beam me up, Scotty"? That was a form of re-membering. The molecules of the person's body would be translated into a code that could be transferred and reconstituted somewhere else. Something like this actually happens when we re-member someone. Our awareness of the person is transferred as neurochemical data into memory cells and with recall this awareness is reconstituted.

Dr. John Polkinghorne, a mathematical physicist at Cambridge University who later became an Anglican priest, hypothesizes that the resurrection of the body may be effected as a function of God's memory.[9] The code that represents us, embedded physically in the molecules of DNA that inhabit each of our cells, is held in God's memory throughout our lives and remains there after we die. When we die, our molecules disorganize and return to dust. At some future point in time, God will "re-member us"—reconstitute us according to the code that he has stored in memory, perhaps after healing the code of any defects it may have picked up along the way.

The apostle Paul spoke of the Communion meal as a meal of "remembrance" (1 Corinthians 11:24–25). This doesn't just mean it's the time we call to mind Jesus and what he's done for us. It's more like the Passover meal, which in the Hebrew understanding was a way for each generation of Israel to participate in the original Passover, when God delivered the Israelites from their bondage in Egypt.

---

9. John Polkinghorne, *The Faith of a Physicist* (Minneapolis: Fortress, 1996), 163–64.

Hold Loved Ones in Memory before Love

To remember someone is to call him from stored memory to conscious awareness, usually with some intention or feeling associated with the recall. Holding loved ones in memory before Love himself is a form of prayer. Call the person to mind and hold him in your mind's eye aware that you are presenting him in love to the source of all love. As your mind wanders to think *about* that person, perhaps analyzing or thinking critically about him, gently return to your intention to simply hold him in your memory in the presence of God's love. Let go of judgment, knowing that each person stands before the judgment seat of Christ, and "the Lord is able to make him stand" (Romans 14:4).

Hold each person in memory for as long as you are able to focus on the person (by which I mean, gently return to focusing on him when your mind wanders), and then move on to the next person.

My friend Donna describes her own practice of the prayer of remembrance:

> One of the things I do is a Quaker prayer practice of "holding people in the Light." I first heard my mother-in-law do this years ago, and the practice has stayed with me. I experience a lot of relief from the burden of having to know how to pray for people in a specific way and a lot of wonder at how God intervenes in peoples' lives. At times I'm a walker when praying, which means that I'll go up and down my hallway or around my living room with my hands out, palms up, "holding someone in the Light." Asking that the Spirit of Christ work in that person according to his or her need, and for the praise of God.

I found that it is best to begin by focusing on the people you hold most dear and with whom you have the least conflict. Stick with those people until your brain learns how to maintain a simple, noncritical focus on them. Then expand the circle to include others. When your brain has been soaked in the calming feelings of love for others, you will be in a better position to eventually pray in this way for those you may not like or with whom you're having serious conflict, even people you regard as enemies.

Occasionally when I'm praying for someone like this, I'll receive a sympathetic understanding of a person's situation; a particular sense of God's love or an encouraging or affirming thing to say to him or her may also be given. A time may come to share that with the person.[10]

Guard Your Heart in Your Core Relationships

You can imagine how this practice can have the effect of guarding your heart toward important people in your life—like close family members, coworkers, and friends.

Married couples, in particular, are subject to something called "stress spillover."[11] The marriage bond is a weight-bearing bond subject to all kinds of demands—financial demands, time demands, the burden of shared responsibilities. This is as it should be. But the stress-bearing capacity of a marriage can come at an emotional cost as we associate our partner with all the challenging things we are facing together.

---

10. When deciding whether to share something like this with someone first ask yourself, "Is this something I would want to hear if I were in his shoes?" (Not just, "Would this be good for him?")

11. R. L. Brock and E. A. Lawrence "A Longitudinal Investigation of Stress Spillover in Marriage: Does Spousal Support Adequately Buffer the Effects?" *Journal of Family Psychology*, 2008 February 22 (1): 11–20.

The teacher of Proverbs offers this wisdom for his sons who are married: "May your fountain be blessed, / and may you rejoice in the wife of your youth. / A loving doe, a graceful deer— / may her breasts satisfy you always, / may you ever be captivated by her love" (Proverbs 5:18–19). Guard your heart toward the important people in your life.

Whatever else the Song of Songs may be, it is an erotic love poem that can be read and pondered meditatively as a way to keep a lover's heart alive to his or her beloved when the relationship is being tested by all the weight it is bearing.

Or try this on for size if you're a married man: meditate on the creation of Eve in the Garden of Eden (Genesis 2:21–23). Read the text slowly three times, then place yourself in the text as Adam (a name which simply means "human"), who has fallen asleep and awakened to the presence of his wife. No words are exchanged between Adam and Eve in this scene. Presumably they spent some time looking at each other. Man, behold your wife! Woman, behold your husband! (The meditation works either way as both Adam and Eve can be thought to "awaken" and are presented by God to each other.)

Meditation Strengthens Compassion

The mystics of the Christian tradition—Ignatius of Loyola, Theresa of Avila, John of the Cross, Catherine of Siena,[12] and others—were known for having an intensified compassion for others. Some, like Julian of Norwich, seemed to be in danger of going overboard in the love department, perhaps even crossing boundaries

---

12. These are just the ones we know because they were known by powerful people. There are many others who were little known, so their stories haven't been told—yet.

of conventional belief for the sake of love. Sometimes the mystical prayer of the mystics made their superiors nervous.

Love respects boundaries but can also push the boundaries of a conventional "orthodoxy" that hasn't been adequately soaked in love—the true *aim* of orthodoxy.[13] Perhaps you've known someone whose faith seems to be dominated by left-brain thinking; the person has a clear grasp of the details of Christian doctrine, but hasn't integrated the right side of the brain, the big-picture, loving, caring, compassionate parts of the brain. Everything about the person's faith seems correct, but something is fundamentally off. What's off may be the aim of faith: love.

> *Love respects boundaries but can also push the boundaries of a conventional "orthodoxy" that hasn't been adequately soaked in love—the true aim of orthodoxy.*

This seems to have been one of the points of controversy between Jesus and the Pharisees. Jesus stressed the role of love in understanding and interpreting the Bible. The Sermon on the Mount was, in part, a critique of the prevailing orthodoxy of the day, heavily influenced by the Pharisees. It's a sermon riddled with a radical vision of love, including this dramatic statement about the Bible: "Therefore, whatever you want men to do to you, do also to them, for this is the Law and the Prophets" (Matthew 7:12 NKJV). This golden rule of love *is* orthodoxy, *is* the Bible. Sounds shocking, doesn't it?

Andrew Newberg and Robert Waldman, researchers at the University of Pennsylvania, have studied the neurological impact of prayer with respect to compassion. When, for example, we

---

13. See William Harmless, *Mystics* (Oxford: Oxford University Press, 2008), 4–7, for an insightful comparison of "scholastic theology" and "mystical theology."

meditate on God's compassion, one of the structures in the brain that mediates compassion is strengthened. This structure lies between the emotional center of the brain (the limbic system) and the logic-reasoning center of the brain (frontal lobe). When these neurons are strengthened by use, the circuit can dampen the effect of powerful emotions that inhibit compassion, like fear. The anterior cingulate cortex is the portion of the brain that is activated when we see others suffer, enabling us to feel compassion.[14]

Prayer Fueled Jesus' Compassion

In the opening chapter of the gospel of Mark, Jesus rises early to pray in solitude (1:35). He then begins a tour of Galilee to preach good news and do the works of the kingdom. In this sequence he is approached by a man with leprosy. "Filled with compassion, Jesus reached out his hand and touched the man" (Mark 1:41). This simple act would have rendered Jesus ritually unclean according to the ritual purity laws, but compassion moved Jesus to touch the man anyway.

We can infer that prayer empowered Jesus with compassion.

Prayer *affects* us. Prayer can strengthen the anterior cingulate cortex, so that we respond with compassion to those in

Prayer empowered Jesus with compassion.

need rather than pulling away in fear. Prayer can increase our capacity for compassion. In fact, this is a good way to measure whether your praying is effective. Is your prayer affecting you in this way? If not, perhaps it's time to try a different way of praying.

---

14. Andrew Newberg, MD, and Mark Robert Waldman, *How God Changes Your Brain* (New York: Ballantine, 2009), 123–27.

The brain seems to be wired to reward our acts of compassion. Scientists have documented a phenomenon called "helper's high."[15] When you do something for someone else—an act of kindness such as offering aid to a homeless person—your brain releases endorphins into your bloodstream, the same chemicals that give a runner a "second wind" or "runner's high." The endorphins are naturally occurring painkillers and mood lifters.

The helper's high is stronger when you help someone who is not part of your kinship group. Not only do you get a burst of endorphins after helping a stranger, but you also receive a second burst of endorphins when you recall helping the stranger. Your brain and your God are trying to tell you, *Well done! Do it again!*

We Are Connected After All

Prayer is a powerful way to put us in touch with the reality that we are profoundly connected, that to be alive is to be embedded in a network of connections. Scripture offers abundant witness to this reality, beginning with the opening chapter of the book of Genesis, which places us within a connected creation—sharing the breath of life with other creatures and the gift of life with all living things (Genesis 1:30). The opening chapters of Genesis are ripe for meditative prayer.

The gospel of John says that Jesus is both the source of our biological life and our spiritual (eternal) life. Both forms of life are marked by connections: between creatures and the Creator, between creatures and creation, and between creatures and each

---

15. Alan Luks and Peggy Payne, *The Healing Power of Doing Good* (Bloomington, IN: iUniverse, 2001).

other. This is reflected in three early Christian expressions of eternal life: the communion of saints, the fellowship of the Spirit, and the cloud of witnesses (mentioned earlier). To participate in "eternal life" is to be part of a communion of saints, a fellowship of the Spirit, and to be surrounded by a cloud of witnesses.

We're never alone, in other words. We're connected, which is what it means to be alive. We are not meant to be alone, isolated, disconnected.[16]

We're never alone, in other words. We're connected, which is what it means to be alive.

There's a place for us on the love network, so long as we are willing to let God be God and let love be love and surrender to love accordingly.

Currently the network, much like the Internet itself, is in a diseased state. Worms and viruses are running rampant all over it, because—well, we're vulnerable to these infections and we're there. We can remain on the network only as long as we are willing to let love heal us—tenderly, gently, patiently, excruciatingly, in whatever way love chooses. All we can do is trust that love, being love, knows best.

Prayer is one of the means of this healing process. Prayer is designed to heal our brains of the effects of excess anger, which seems to be especially hard on the neurons. The nerves involved in anger even look jagged and rough. The bonds they form are strong. While there is a legitimate place for anger, there are strong warnings regarding its power to harm. In this vein, James, the brother of Jesus said, "The anger of man does not achieve the righteousness of God" (James 1:20 NASB).

So much religion these days seems to generate and feed on

---

16. Whatever hell is, it is a sorrowful place of disconnection so difficult to imagine that every attempt simply terrifies us.

anger. That kind of religion is bad for our brains.[17] It doesn't get the righteousness of God done, that's for sure. We should pay extra attention to engaging in prayer practices that calm our angry brains and help them forgive ourselves and others, let go of hurts, and leave the judging to God, who has enough love to handle wrath without being consumed by it.

We struggle in prayer, of course. Life is a struggle for existence. But to pray—every single time and every single attempt—is to confess that we are connected.

---

17. Gordon Allport, in *The Individual and His Religion* (New York: MacMillan, 1967), distinguishes between "extrinsic religion," which is more self-centered, viewing religion as a means to an end; and "intrinsic religion," which is more concerned with others and the whole of life; the latter was seen to contribute to the health of the individual but not the former.

SIX

Calming: Praying to Tame the Worry Dog

I hadn't felt it like this before: an attack of *something* that seemed to come on like a storm. At first, I became unusually aware of my breathing. *Hmm, why am I paying attention to my breathing? I'm not out of breath, or shouldn't be. Or am I?*[1]

Then I noticed an interior buzzing, like a copper wire carrying too much current. *What's got me so worked up?*

My thoughts became confused. My synapses felt slightly out of sync. *And a one and a two: why can't I get my thoughts into a better rhythm? Am I going to faint? That's not possible, is it? Maybe I should get up and move around. Or lie down. Maybe I should get out of this shrinking room. Maybe all I need is a little fresh air. Maybe there's too much carbon monoxide in this place. Is that why I feel so strange?*

Ten minutes into this thing, it occurred to me: *This might be a panic attack. My dad had panic attacks. I had no idea they could*

---

1. Later, I learned that there is a smothering reflex in the brain that can register a false positive. You think you're smothering or might be on the verge of smothering, so you become hypervigilant about your breathing.

be this unpleasant. Maybe I don't need to call the ambulance. There doesn't seem to be anything wrong with me. But why would I feel more secure in an ambulance right now, rushing to the ER?

Yep, I think this must be a panic attack.

It had been a stressful week. In fact it was the end of a fourteen-day work stretch. I had to squeeze in a last-minute set of meetings with a potential funder for our budding environmental steward-ship ministry. We were just wrapping things up when I started to feel a little strange.

The strange feeling began when I realized that I had to leave for the airport to fly to the Arctic by way of Oslo with a group of high-powered people I didn't know. *What was I doing on a trip with a guest list that includes celebrities? I must have been invited by mistake!*

I may have to cancel this trip. No. I'll be okay. This is a panic attack. People don't die from panic attacks. I'm going to be fine. This too shall pass.

The attack did, in fact, go away after about an hour. I was rattled, but fine.

Panic is simply worry on steroids.

What, Me Worry?

We worry because we can. So far as we know, worms can't worry. They blithely burrow through the dirt in search of . . . more dirt. They live in the now, whereas we spend much of our mental energy imagining the future. We burrow through life with a fur-rowed brow, our frontal lobes forward, conjuring with them what might be but isn't yet. Apparently many of us believe that more things can go wrong than can go right.

If we don't have something we need, we worry that we won't get it. If we do have it, we worry that we'll lose it.

As the self-absorbed song goes: "It's not easy being me!"[2] (Or you, either, I'll bet.)

Don't blame yourself. Blame your frontal lobe—the part of the human brain that makes us wise (*Homo sapiens* means "man the wise"). Wise, as in able to anticipate the future and act in the present accordingly. Squirrels bury acorns for the winter by instinct, but we sow seeds to reap a coming harvest by planning for the future.

We do this cogitating with the part of the brain that makes our heads large enough to cause our mothers pain in the process of giving birth to us. This should be a clue that our big brains are a mixed blessing.

We Come from a Long Line of Alert People

Worry is a form of fear connected to the alarm system of our brains. Many of us have an overactive alarm system. This makes perfect sense when you consider that all of our direct ancestors had an alarm system that worked well enough to keep them alive long enough to breed.[3] We come from a long line of alert people.

The brain's alarm system is called the stress response. It is activated in the presence of any danger or threat, including events perceived as blocking the attainment of a goal.[4] The body's stress response includes the following:

- Acceleration of heart-rate and breathing
- Inhibition of gastrointestinal function
- Constriction of blood vessels in many parts of the body

---

2. "It's Not Easy to Be Me," lyrics by David Gray.
3. Each person alive is alive only because all of his or her direct ancestors managed to live long enough to pass on their DNA to their offspring.
4. Pierce J. Howard, PhD, *The Owner's Manual for the Brain*, 3rd ed., "The Anatomy of Stress" (Austin, TX: Bard Press, 2006), 314–20.

- Release of nutrients for muscular action
- Expansion of blood vessels for large muscles
- Dry eyes and mouth
- Dilation of the pupils to enhance vision in the dark
- Relaxation of the bladder (and other "now is not the time" effects)
- Inhibition of erection

This response is sometimes called the "fight-flight-freeze response" because it prompts us to do one of three things in response to a perceived threat: fight it off, run from it, or freeze until we can decide what the threat is.[5]

The response can be mild or severe, and it can be triggered by any danger or threat, real or imagined. The brain takes time to distinguish between real and imagined threats, and by that time, the alarm system is already firing. Just thinking about a danger or threat can trigger the body's stress response.

The stress response is designed to stimulate rapid bursts of intense physical activity. But our capacity to *imagine* threats subjects our bodies to the stress response even though there's nothing to do but stew in our alarm juices. It wears us out prematurely, like a copper penny soaked in acid.

Prayer can calm or stimulate the stress response, depending on how we pray.

How can prayer make it worse? You guessed it—in many different ways! We can pray for others by focusing on what's wrong with them and thus stimulate our alarm system. We can pray and worry that we're not praying enough. We can nurse

---

5. The "freeze" response is the initial response of deer who detect an early and unknown threat, the proverbial "deer in the headlights" response.

perceived offenses while we pray. We can, in short, do a lot of fussing in prayer.

Many devout believers feel completely defeated about their prayer lives because for them, prayer is just another space to worry in.

How do we pray in such a way that we tame rather than inflame the worry dog that seems to be barking so annoyingly inside?

In this chapter, we will focus on three things: praying through troubling situations, focusing on the good around us, and meditating on scripture. In chapter 8, we'll consider how to relax so as to pray more effectively, which also helps us deal with worry.

Pray Your Way Through Troubling Circumstances

Several of the New Testament letters deal with relational stress within the early Jesus communities, a form of stress that prompts much of our own worry. For example:

> I plead with Euodia and I plead with Syntyche to be of the same mind in the Lord. Yes, and I ask you, my true companion, help these women since they have contended at my side in the cause of the gospel, along with Clement and the rest of my co-workers, whose names are in the book of life. (Philippians 4:2–3 TNIV)

Disputes between leaders of a community are perceived by the community as a threat to their well-being, stimulating the stress response.

When I was about ten years old, I had a recurring night terror in which massive blocks were grinding against each other; just this nameless, abstract dread. I didn't tell anyone about it—how could

I if I couldn't even put it into words? It was 1962, the year of the Cuban Missile Crisis, when the United States and the Soviet Union came close to nuclear war. It was also a time when my parents' marriage was under intense pressures that were unknown to me at the time. I was the passive observer of simmering conflict between two parties, and it was stimulating my fight-flight response, but there was no one to fight and nowhere to run.

The source of a threat may be external, but it changes our inner world. As John Milton put it, "The mind is its own place, and in itself / can make a Heaven of Hell, a Hell of Heaven."[6] Our guard dog is barking; our worry dog is whimpering; our body defenses are alert: our blood pressure is elevated, our hands are cold, and we feel queasy while blood is diverted from the gut to the extremities.

The source of a threat may be external, but it changes our inner world.

After appealing to the leaders in conflict to settle their dispute, Paul addressed the community's anxiety:

> Rejoice in the Lord always. I will say it again: Rejoice! Let your gentleness be evident to all. The Lord is near. Do not be anxious about anything, but in every situation, by prayer and petition, with thanksgiving, present your requests to God. And the peace of God, which transcends all understanding, will guard your hearts and your minds in Christ Jesus. (Philippians 4:4–7 TNIV)

Much of what we call worry is rumination, rehearsing a negative emotion, event, or anticipated outcome—often for an extended period.

---

6. John Milton, *Paradise Lost*, Book 1, line 22.

Since I'm high on verbal skills, I can ruminate for a long time over an upcoming conversation that might be laden with conflict, imagining a cogent defense to every conceivable verbal parry and thrust. Rumination is fueled by the alarm system and, in turn, further stimulates it. Thus it is one of the most harmful feedback loops we can experience.

Paul was advocating an awareness shift. Turn from a focus on the threat to a focus on some blessing or resource in the midst of the threat. This shift is modeled in the twenty-third Psalm: "You prepare a table before me in the presence of my enemies . . . my cup overflows" (Psalm 23:5). The shift in focus triggers the brain's calming system.[7]

The church leaders in conflict (Euodia and Syntyche) needed to calm down. The church alarmed by their conflict needed to calm down. Paul, who seemed to have had an active alarm system himself,[8] knew that a certain kind of praying can help.

This shift is intentional, and requires effort to execute. It takes practice. Every time we practice making this shift, we reinforce the pathways that make the shift easier in much the same way that we develop muscle memory by practicing an athletic, musical, or manual skill.

Practice Makes Easy

Picture a golf swing. The golfer first addresses the ball. Looking to the flag on the green, she lines up her body along the axis she wants the ball to travel. Next comes the backswing, arms extended and the club raised, poised for the downswing when

---

7. The alarm system of the brain involves the sympathetic nervous system (SNS), and the calming system involves the parasympathetic nervous system (PNS).

8. See, for example 2 Corinthians 12:20–21 and Philippians 2:28.

Think of prayer as one fluid motion with these three components: orienting your heart Godward, making your requests known, and pivoting your focus.

the golfer pivots her hips just as the club face strikes the ball, transferring the full weight of the swing to the ball.

A golf swing is one fluid motion with three components: the address, the backswing, and the downswing with pivot.

Think of prayer as one fluid motion with these three components: orienting your heart Godward, making your requests known, and pivoting your focus from the threat to the blessings present in the midst of the threat.

Addressing the Ball Is Orienting Your Heart Godward

When you're worried about something, address it by turning to God for help! I'm amazed that after all these years, I still forget that I can ask God for help when faced with challenges.

Ruminating worry is a dark room with no windows. It's easy to forget that there's an outside world beyond your worry—that the sun may be shining outside despite the gloom inside. You have to break out of the confining space of worry by *exerting the intention* to orient your heart Godward. This is what the psalmist was doing when he said, "In the day of trouble I will call to you" (Psalm 86:7).

Why did the psalmist make a point to state his intention? Why didn't he just do it? Because he knew by experience that in order to "just do it" he had to first make the conscious effort of intention. He had to summon himself to do it.

Like the golfer addressing the ball because she intends to take a swing at the ball, take stock of your situation in light of the possibility that God may be able to help. Aim your heart in that new direction. This intention of yours can be expressed in a simple word of address, like "Father." This seems to have been Jesus' favorite way of addressing God (in the form of Hebrew that Jesus spoke, Aramaic, it was *Abba*.)

You can take a deep breath and pause for a moment on that word of address: *Father*, or in the very words of Jesus, *Abba*.

The Backswing Is Putting Your Request into Words

Next comes the backswing: putting your request into words. Once you've oriented your heart toward God, formulate a specific request for assistance. The process of putting a request into words allows us to step back from the rumination to decide what a more productive approach might be. What could we ask God for in light of this troubling situation? Because rumination is such an introspective activity, it helps to externalize the request by speaking it aloud.

When rumination is running amok, it may be helpful to talk things over with someone else so you can more easily put your thoughts into words and formulate a request that you can make together with the aid of a fellow pray-er.

In the process, you're more likely to consider other responses besides fear-based responses: forgiveness, tolerance, compassion, loving confrontation, and so on. Together you can join in prayer for the situation. Anything that can help you externalize the process, including writing the request down on paper, is helpful.

The Downswing-Pivot Is Shifting from Asking to Thanking

A golf swing is possible without pivoting the hips, but it's not very effective. In fact, the pivot is the crucial aspect of a powerful swing; the pivot transfers the full force of the swing to the ball.

Shifting your focus from fear to thanksgiving does the same

thing. Surround your asking with the practice of focused attention on those things you have reason to be thankful for. It will calm you in the face of worry.

All gratitude requires focused attention. Is the glass half full or half empty? It depends on which part of the glass you are focused on. The fact is, we do have more things to be thankful for than we focus our sustained attention on. The more we focus our attention on the things we have to be thankful for, the more thankful we feel. Not rocket science; neuroscience.

All gratitude requires focused attention.

The shift in focus is like a crack in the door that lets God in: *Maybe I'm not alone; maybe there's help; maybe we—God and I and the others who care about me—can get through this together.*

As the American auto companies have lost value, my home state, Michigan, has suffered steady job loss in this important sector of our economy for the past nine years. When the global recession hit in 2008, it hit our church hard—giving was down 18 percent in the first quarter of our fiscal year.

I was worried. I went to sleep worried, woke up worried, and woke up in the middle of the night worried. Life was a worry-fest for a while.

I can still remember the relief I experienced talking over our financial situation with our church board. These are men and women I love and trust. I'm glad they are in charge of our finances.

They had all been through lean financial times themselves, personally and in their businesses. And like so many businesspeople I know who are devoted followers of Jesus, they had developed a robust faith for God's provision in lean financial times.

The woman who served as our church treasurer had a particular gift of trust in this area. It turns out that she had composed a specific prayer for God to provide financially for the needs of her family, the poor and needy, and our church. This prayer was written down and tucked away in her Bible. When I learned of it, I said, "Could you make that prayer available to us?" Lynne gave me a copy and I tucked it away in my Bible and used it. The prayer was laced with thanksgiving.

It's no surprise that Lynne was always the first to express thanks for the generous provision of finances God provided for our church. Even when the income was running behind, Lynne was quick to express gratitude for the money that had been given.

Lynne had learned the power of the pivot: shifting the focus from the need at hand (which necessarily recognizes the present lack) to the things we have to be thankful for.

The Result Is a Peace That Transcends the Alarm System

Let's give the brain's alarm system the credit it deserves. Worry is trying to guard us. That's the purpose of the stress response. But with all that barking by the worry dog, it's difficult to get a good night's sleep. Even when a real guard dog barks to alert his sleeping humans to a real intruder, there comes a time when the dog needs to stop barking—you're alerted already and calling 911, but the operator can't hear you for all the barking!

But there is another guard on duty, the peace of God that transcends understanding, which guards our hearts and minds. This was not prayer theory for Paul but his steady practice. Earlier in the letter to the Philippians, he wrote, "I thank my God upon every remembrance of you, always in every prayer of mine making request for you all with joy" (1:3–4 NKJV). He worried about the churches, but he kept worry at bay by praying with thanksgiving.

You can try it on an emergency basis. But it's better to treat this practice like yeast that you knead into the lump of the dough that is your prayer life. Make it a habit to pray this way—combine asking with focused gratitude as often as you ask.

We Can't Get Enough of That Focused Attention

Paul reinforced the power of thanksgiving with these closing words: "Finally, brothers and sisters, whatever is true, whatever is noble, whatever is right, whatever is pure, whatever is lovely, whatever is admirable—if anything is excellent or praiseworthy—think about such things. Whatever you have learned or received or heard from me, or seen in me—put it into practice. And the God of peace will be with you" (Philippians 4:8–9 TNIV).

Focused attention on the good makes a huge difference in prayer. Paul understood that when we're buffeted by worry, we have to go searching for any scrap of something good to focus on. We must make a *concerted effort* to dwell on the good.

You're looking for a place to exert effort in prayer? You want to try hard? Try hard here. Worry is an active form of pessimism. We can turn from worry only by putting our focus on the good.

Have you ever enjoyed something that others don't? Don't you want to say to the person who doesn't enjoy what you find so enjoyable, "Let me show you how to enjoy this; you're missing the beauty, the fun, the pleasure!"

I don't enjoy NASCAR, so I did a little thought experiment to see if I could learn to appreciate it. What do people see in NASCAR? All I see is monotony—people driving fast in circles. But they see something else.

They see, perhaps the simplicity and closure that NASCAR brings: a race with a beginning, a middle, and clear outcome. It has drama: dangers to overcome, winners and losers. And teamwork—

the pit stops and the crew working together. NASCAR involves a set of interlocking dependencies: car on driver, driver on car, car and driver on the pit crew, and so on.

See there? I'm talking myself into *liking* NASCAR, and I haven't even focused on the sensory experience: the smell of burning rubber, the roar of the crowd, the hot dogs and the long lines at the porta-potties—ah, see? The brain is a pessimist if we lose our focus.

The brain shaped by an overactive alarm system becomes a raging pessimist in fact: *There's more bad than good to focus on! Life is ruled by Murphy's Law! You have a lot of threats around here, and that's why I have to do so much barking!*

Is that true? That's for us to decide. Based on the evidence, you can make the case either way. But there's also a sixth sense called faith—one that takes evidence like Jesus of Nazareth into account.

If by this sixth sense we discern that God is good, then the universe he created, for all its threats to our safety, is good. And we have a share in the goodness of God and his universe. And life, for all its distress, is good.

If God is good, then focusing on the good isn't naïve. Focusing on the good isn't just what some corny-prone people do to make themselves feel better, but the saps don't realize it's all a big fiction. To focus on the good . . . to look for it, and once you've spotted it, to attend to it, is to catch a glimpse of the goodness of God.

Julian of Norwich crafted a prayer that is based on this understanding that good will prevail, because God is good, and God will prevail. The prayer goes like this: "All shall be well, and all shall be well, and all manner of things shall be well." If you're a worrywart, you might want to memorize this prayer and commit it to regular use.

Focused Attention Is a Meditative Practice

Focused attention is a meditative practice, and it's no accident that meditation is at the heart of the various forms of prayer that calm the brain's alarm system. This is reflected in the New King James Version of Philippians 4:8: "meditate on these things."

The part of our brain responsible for concentrated focus can handle only four to seven bits of information at a time. Jonah Lehrer, in his book *How We Decide*, emphasizes the limits of the late-arriving frontal lobe, the part of our brain that calculates and concentrates. In one test, a group of subjects received two numbers to remember. A second group had to remember seven numbers. When both groups were presented with two different snacks—a calorie-rich chocolate cake or a healthy bowl of fruit— those who had seven bits of data had less willpower available to pass on the cake in favor of the fruit.[9] This may be why your kids wait until your brain is overloaded to ask you for a treat—they know it's easier for you to say, "Oh, why not?" when your frontal lobe is occupied.

The part of your brain that can become easily fatigued with too many bits of information to handle at one time is also the part of the brain that helps us to practice meditative prayer. The most common method of meditative prayer is to give focused attention to one thing at a time, or better yet, for an extended period of time. When we do this (and it can take practice), we can actually quiet the running chatter that is such a distraction to prayer.

The best way to quiet the running monologue of our left hemisphere is not to tell it to be quiet, but to focus instead on one thing for an extended period. This allows some of the functions

---

9. Jonah Lehrer, *How We Decide* (Boston: Houghton, Mifflin, Harcourt, 2009), 150–52.

of the right brain to exert themselves. These functions include a sense of calm and peace and connection with the wider world, including God.

What's Your Intention?

This is where intention comes in again. It normally takes the effort of conscious intention to meditate, but it also takes the effort of intention to decide how to direct one's meditation. This simple method of meditation can be calming whether or not the person meditating is even focused on God. You can focus on a leaf, a stone, or a candle and thereby calm your mind. We can meditate without praying, and we can pray meditatively without aiming our hearts toward God.

It's up to each of us to aim our hearts—or to use the biblical language, to turn our hearts—toward something or someone. Whenever we pray, including when we pray meditatively, it's our intention that aims our hearts. As a follower of Jesus, my intention in practicing meditative prayer is to open myself to Jesus and his Spirit. This intention, I believe, has a big influence on the shaping of my mind in prayer. It really does matter who or what we focus on.

> Whenever we pray, including when we pray meditatively, it's our intention that aims our hearts.

Recently neuroscientists have learned the importance of certain brain cells called "mirror neurons." When you smile at me and I smile back, it's because your smile gets my smiling mirror neurons firing.[10] In conversation with others, we tend to

---

10. V. S. Ramachandran, *A Brief Tour of Consciousness* (New York: PI Press, 2004), 37–39.

mirror the speech patterns and gestures of the people we are focusing our attention on. In fact, mirror neurons are so powerful that if there weren't a part of our brain specifically designed to override their impact, we would simply act out what we see other people doing.

We tend to become like whatever it is that we worship. The intention of our hearts in meditative prayer makes a great difference indeed.

You Can Do It

With practice, the brain *can* be trained to focus attention on one thing at a time. Select a word, phrase, text, or image as your focal point. It might be something as simple as a word for God (Father, Savior, Lord) or a visual or other sensory image from a psalm. When you begin this kind of prayer, it's easiest to select something that your heart is already drawn to. Decide how long you'd like to focus your attention on that one thing (for example, three, five, ten, or twenty minutes) then turn your attention to that one word, phrase, or image.

As distracting thoughts intrude—and they normally will—gently return your focus to the one thing.

It is important to treat distractions *gently*. They are inevitable, like flies on a hot summer day. Except there's no use swatting away distractions. In fact, distractions *like* the attention, so getting angry or frustrated or annoyed by the distracting thoughts only encourages them to linger. Even the mild annoyance that comes with noticing that your mind has wandered will focus your attention *more* on the distraction itself. Simply *notice* the presence of a distracting thought and gently redirect your focused attention to the intended focus of your meditation.

You *Must* Adopt a Nonjudgmental Approach to Distractions

This is really important: you *must* take a nonjudgmental approach to the fact that you will get distracted. *Of course* your mind will wander. *Of course* you will lose your focus. Don't be upset when this happens. What good will that do? None. It will only direct your focus even more to the distraction.

Don't judge yourself. Gently redirect your focus back to your original intention.

Again and again.

At first, it may feel like you are *constantly* redirecting your focus to your original intention. It's like learning to pronounce someone's foreign-sounding name, the sound of which you can barely make out, let alone pronounce. If you really want to learn how to pronounce her name, you may have to ask her to repeat it and then attempt to say it several times. It's a little humbling, isn't it? But over time, it works. The brain makes and reinforces the connections.

Think of it: every time you return to your focus, the connection between the neurons involved is strengthened so that it takes less stimulation to keep the connection going. That's how neural connections work. Once the pathway is established, it's easier to keep it open, just like a path through the woods.

Meditation requires the persistent willingness to gently redirect your attention as often as you need to.

Meditation requires the *persistent willingness* to gently redirect your attention as often as you need to away from distracting thoughts to the one thing you've chosen to focus on. This requires more effort on the front end, but it pays in the long run. Believe that.

Remember, focused attention is so powerful that it can help a woman get through the stress and pain of childbirth, especially when combined with relaxing breathing techniques.

For each of her five deliveries, my wife, Nancy, focused on a cross that we placed on the wall in her line of sight. I even used it a few times myself when things were getting a little nerve-racking. You don't need to know about the time I nearly passed out from doing the breathing techniques as my wife's "coach" (imagine a baseball coach who has never played the game!). Apparently, I didn't need the extra oxygen like she did.

Meditate on Scripture

Scripture is *designed* for mediation. These are living words that we are meant to enter through meditation. They are revelatory, light-bathed, God-breathed words that can lead us into God's presence. What's the sense in believing in the inspiration of Scripture if you don't believe *that*?

Allow me to belabor this point. It's not just that the words of scripture can be used for meditation. They are *meant* to be used for meditation. This is one of the things scripture is *for*. Remember that scripture came into existence well before the printing press made copies available to a wide audience. Only wealthy people had their own copies of the handwritten scrolls of scripture. Instead, most people heard the scripture read aloud, rather than reading it themselves. In order to use scripture, people had to memorize what they heard. Memorization is a form of meditation and in turn allows the person who has committed the scripture to memory to later meditate on it.

One of my New Testament professors said that the Beatitudes at the beginning of the Sermon on the Mount were composed to be memorable; in the original Aramaic that Jesus spoke, it is likely they had a rhythmic cadence not unlike rap lyrics today. Jesus used language that was colorful, vivid, attention-grabbing, memorable, and pleasing to the ear. He used words designed to penetrate the heart—or as the author of Hebrews says, "piercing even to the division of soul and spirit, and of joints and marrow" (Hebrews 4:12 NKJV). Meditation is what allows these words to soak in.

The Hebrew word for *meditate* can also be translated "murmur." The process of memorization is perhaps the simplest form of meditation—repeating the text over and over. Meditation can be done out loud or silently. It begins as simply as repeating a word or phrase over and over.

There are many different ways to meditate on scripture, but all of them have one thing in common: slow down!

There are many different ways to meditate on scripture, but all of them have one thing in common: slow down! Speed-reading is for cheap novels and boring textbooks, not scripture. The words of scripture are "more precious than gold, than much pure gold; they are sweeter than honey, than honey from the comb" (Psalm 19:10). Honey in the Middle East was a rare treat—a sticky sweetness that clings to the tongue, lips, and fingers. You can't swallow it quickly even if you want to. It's designed to linger.

Here's a simple method for meditating on scripture.

1. Select a small portion of scripture—nothing longer than the Twenty-Third Psalm. To begin, select something you are already familiar with and that your heart is already drawn to.

2. Read your selected portion of scripture over slowly. Repeat a second time, and a third. As you read the text, look for a word, phrase, image, or scene that your heart is drawn to. By this I mean, pay attention to the subtle inner response you have as you read the text. A particular scene, word, or phrase may stand out from the rest of the text.

Since meditating on scripture is different than studying scripture, try to focus on the feeling aspects of the text, even something as basic as the sound of the words and what the words evoke in you. This is not the time for careful critical analysis of the text. Though study of the scripture can enhance our meditation, studying scripture and meditating on scripture are different activities.

It's a bit like listening to music: what feelings does the sound evoke in you, what mood does it generate, what are the movements of your heart in response to the music? Note even subtle responses to the text: curiosity, interest—any attractive tug.

3. Once you have identified a portion of the text that is already moving your heart, even in a very subtle way, focus on that portion—a word, phrase, or image—as the one thing you decide to meditate on.

If you are new to meditating on scripture, it can help to begin with a text loaded with visual imagery like Psalm 23:

> *The Lord is my shepherd, I shall not be in want.*
> *He makes me lie down in green pastures,*
> *he leads me beside quiet waters,*
> *he restores my soul.*
> *He guides me in paths of righteousness,*
> *for his name's sake.*

Even though I walk
  through the valley of the shadow of death,
I will fear no evil,
  for you are with me;
your rod and your staff,
  they comfort me.
You prepare a table for me
  in the presence of my enemies.
You anoint my head with oil;
  my cup overflows.
Surely goodness and love will follow me
  all the days of my life,
and I will dwell in the house of the LORD
  forever.

Perhaps your heart was drawn to the image of lying down in green pastures beside still waters. Good. Read that portion over again slowly.

He makes me lie down in green pastures,
he leads me beside quiet waters,
  he restores my soul.

Read it a second time, and a third. A fourth if you like.

Now place yourself within the scene using your imagination.

Did You Say, "Use Your Imagination"?

Some Christians are nervous about the word *imagination*. I suppose they think of it as a kind of fantasy that takes us further away from reality. And they know that God is the real God, not the unreal one.

But words are useless without the imagination. Repeat: useless. Words are nothing if not a code meant to *stimulate* the imagination. I say "tree" and you imagine a tree, or else the word *tree* hasn't worked. Without the imagination we are unable to engage reality in the unique way that we are meant to as those who carry the image of God. Nothing against worms, per se, but worms are not imaginative creatures. We are.

This is especially true of the vivid word pictures we have in the Twenty-Third Psalm. To receive these words of scripture is to picture the scene—a person lying down in green pastures, being led beside quiet waters.

So imagine that you are part of the scene that the words invite you to imagine. Notice the greenness of the pasture. Feel the texture of the grass as you lie down in it. Stay there for a while in the grass. Notice the smells. Feel the warmth of the sun.

As your mind wanders, *gently* return your attention to the scene to soak it in some more. Then move on to the next portion, the quiet waters . . .

You get the picture. This is what it means to meditate on scripture. It is a form of focused attention, and the effect can be very calming.

Look for a Few Reliable Scriptures to Meditate On

I have a few "in-a-pinch" scriptures to meditate on when I'm stressed. "Be still, and know that I am God" (Psalm 46:10) is one. The Twenty-Third Psalm is another.

Psalm 23 is on my "in-a-pinch list" because I associate this psalm with my father. He told me that the day he was injured in

World War II—November 11, 1944—was the day of the biggest shelling in the war to that date. He was right in the thick of it as a nineteen-year-old sergeant with a radio pack on his back, which was like carrying a big target.

At the time, my father was not very devout, but as he ran across a shallow stream, with shells exploding all around him, he found himself *shouting* the Twenty-Third Psalm out loud, word for word. Amazing the things you retain from Sunday school! On the other side of the stream, he threw himself down at the base of a tree as a mortar shell landed nearby. It killed the soldier on his immediate right and on his immediate left. A fragment ripped through the back of his helmet, was diverted upward, and came out the front without harming his head. Another fragment struck the back of his knee, an injury that got him off the battlefield and may have saved his life.

Many years later, my father lay dying in my home. I was away at the time and my sister Nancy was caring for him. He was having a terrible time—in and out of consciousness, confused, struggling. My sister was beside herself, so she took a break and went to the living room to calm down. She found a Bible and opened to Psalm 23 and read it silently for comfort, then returned to my father's bedside. He opened his eyes in a lucid moment and said, "Even though I walk through the valley of the shadow of death, the Lord is with me. It's going to be all right, Nancy." Shortly, thereafter, he lost consciousness for the last time and died.

God knows that life in this world can be hard. But he has given us brains that can be calmed.

God knows that life in this world can be hard. But he has given us brains that can be calmed, even when the alarm is stuck on.

SEVEN

At Intervals:
Meeting God in Time

Prayer changes things, and chief among the things prayer changes is our brain. Not long ago, we assumed that the brain was set in its ways during childhood. Like a computer without upgrade options, the brain toiled away, we thought, processing new information with the hardware of yesteryear.[1]

Wrong. Happily wrong. The brain, it turns out, is flexible, pliable, supple, adaptable, adjustable, or what the cognitive scientists call "plastic." The brain changes incrementally, with small influences over time, all the time. We change along with it.

As a time-lapse video of any growing thing demonstrates, the dynamism of life is stupefying—constantly adapting, shifting,

---

1. This distorted view of the brain is partly the consequence of thinking of ourselves as machines (like a computer, for example). The brain is often compared to a computer, but we are not computers. We are biological (and by faith, eternal) life forms, mysteries—as is God, in whose image we are created.

changing. Nature changes "all by itself,"[2] interacting with the rest of nature, and by faith, with and under nature's God. The brain functions like an open source software program, but it can also reprogram itself. Every day, changes are being made in the brain as we interact with the world around us.

Consider what this means! What seem like fleeting, insubstantial things—thoughts—are actually dynamic somethings that involve certain nerve cells and not others firing, forming and strengthening new connections, enhancing neural pathways that make it easier to think the same thoughts in the future.

The thoughts we think in turn change the brain that does the thinking. This sheds a whole new light on Paul's words, "think about such things" (Philippians 4:8). What the old wisdom of Scripture has known for ages, the new wisdom of science is affirming.

The relatively new field of "positive psychology" stresses the power of gratitude. The mere act of pausing a few times a week to write down a few things that you are thankful for can increase your brain's capacity for happiness.[3]

The implications for prayer are enormous. Prayer involves shifting our focus of attention—the focus of our thoughts, feelings, mind, heart, and body—toward God and away from other things, or toward other things in the light of God.

God is with us and around us and beyond us whether we pray or not, but prayer signals our intention to acknowledge and make ourselves present to God. Because God is a relational and personal being, this matters, not just to us, but also to him.

In prayer, we say or sing or chant words that express this intention, and this helps us to refocus our attention in a Godward

---

2. This is one of the observations on nature made by Jesus in the parable of the man who planted seed and while he slept the seed sprouted. "All by itself, the soil produces grain—first the stalk, then the head, then the full kernel in the head." (Mark 4:28)

3. Sonja Lyubomirsky, *The How of Happiness* (New York: Penguin, 2007), 91–92.

direction. This time of focused attention results in strengthened neural pathways in our brains. Prayer changes the brain that prays.

Over Time, That Is

The changes that take place in the brain are subtle, and they occur over time. This is why the scientists use the term *plastic* to describe the brain's capacity for change. Plastic bends, but it also resists bending, so steady pressure is required to change its shape. The brain changes like this as well. It can change, but by degrees, *over time*.

You've probably noticed that it takes extra effort to form a new habit, but once the habit is formed, the extra effort is not required. That's the beauty of habits, in fact. They take a while to form, but once formed they allow us to do certain things with *less* effort.

We form habits precisely because we only have a limited amount of mental effort to exert. Certain portions of the brain get tired like the rest of the body. We have to ration our mental energy. Habits help us do this. Because I have the habit of brushing my teeth every morning, I don't have to spend mental energy in order to make myself do it. I can spend that effort on other things.

We may complain about how difficult it is to form new habits, but if we could form habits *too* easily, we'd be in trouble. Habits once formed are difficult to break.

Consider a bad habit like smoking. You don't become a smoker by smoking one cigarette. It takes time.

I smoked my first cigarette when my brother-in-law came over to visit once a week or so. As a gag, I'd smoke one of his cigarettes and cough and get dizzy and tell him he was crazy to smoke. Then I started looking forward to his visits so I could bum a cigarette. After a few months of this, I was working alone at the community mental health center. I felt a little sleepy and needed a boost, so I bought my first pack of cigarettes.

After opening the pack and smoking the first cigarette, I thought, *I'm a smoker now! That means now will be the easiest time to quit.* I threw the rest of the pack away and stopped bumming them off my brother-in-law. I was a one-pack-a-lifetime smoker and quit.

A habit like smoking takes time to form: one cigarette at a time at intervals over time, time after time. Prayer is like that too.

Remember, *it's the brain, stupid!* (You know I'm kidding.) The brain is plastic, which means that it admits small degrees of change at a time over time: one step, one prayer at a time over time. Don't fight it; work with it.

God in Time

Time is the modern bugaboo of prayer. So much practical teaching about prayer stresses the need to "take time for prayer," while the people receiving the teaching protest, "I don't have the time to give!"

In anticipation of this resistance, the teacher marshals many arguments to convince people how important prayer is. Everyone leaves even more frustrated.

Let's step back from that conversation and consider God in time. It is, after all, his invention. The first line of the first book of the Bible is about God in time: "In the beginning, God . . ."[4]

---

4. The first chapter of the book of Genesis is a much misunderstood and misused portion of Scripture. It was gathered into written form long before the scientific method was invented as a way of knowing. The attempt to read it as a piece of "creation science," is to force-fit the text into a modern framework. This modernist reading detracts from what Genesis is: a work of Spirit-inspired writing designed to orient us to ourselves and to God and to our surroundings and our fellow creatures, all in the context of the first mystery it introduces: time.

These opening words entice us to do what we seek to do when we pray: to meet God in time. God may be above and beyond time, but these first words of Genesis bear witness to his presence *in* time.

The creative activity of God takes place in Genesis chapter 1, and often throughout Scripture, emergently, progressively, and incrementally—in other words, over time. In Genesis chapter 1, God orchestrates creation over seven diurnal movements,[5] each day's creativity unfolding in a kind of rhythmic pattern, each iteration building on and adapting

> *God may be above and beyond time, but these first words of Genesis bear witness to his presence in time.*

from what came before, as a musical pattern does. When we tap our feet to a melody, we're hardly "keeping time" since time refuses to be kept. Instead, we're doing the only thing time allows us to do: mark its passing at intervals.

Prayer at Intervals: Daily, Weekly, Seasonally

Subtly, indirectly, surreptitiously even, Genesis chapter 1 draws us into prayer by introducing us to time's sacred rhythms. This is our field guide to nature, including time, and God is right in the middle of it. We have to pay attention to many different things as we make our way through the world because it is a happening place, but wouldn't it be good from time to time to pause to pay special attention to God in time?

Prayer is one of the ways we tend to God in time. Prayer helps us to see the full smorgasbord of life in the light of God in time. Prayer is how we mark time with God.

---

5. "And it was evening, and it was morning, first day." (Genesis 1:5 ALTER)

By doing so, we trace neural pathways for God in our brains. Having prayed once, it is easier to pray twice, and so on. Like other pathways, our prayers facilitate our travel toward, alongside, and under God in time.

Ancient Wisdom: Neurologically Savvy

What do we make of the fact that so many religious traditions mark time in daily, weekly, and seasonal patterns? Prayers in particular are offered daily, weekly, and seasonally. There's a common wisdom at work here, isn't there? Common wisdom doesn't occur by accident. Often it reflects what works, what fits, what makes sense for who we are and how we function. It is neurologically savvy.

It's easy to think of tradition as a set of expectations handed down to us that we are forced by social pressure to keep: like your grandmother's quilts that you never really liked but you can't throw away because you have to pass them on to your children. Say your prayers before bed, go to church, and show up for the family holiday meals to keep Grandma happy.

But what if at least some ancient traditions reflect workable wisdom arrived at by thousands of years of trial and error so that it survives down through the ages because it is so well suited to how we function? What if some of this wisdom is neurologically savvy?

We'd give it a little more respect, wouldn't we? *Did you hear about the study where several different cultures over several thousands of years attempted various ways of praying and discovered that daily, weekly, and seasonally works best?* We take vitamin C to stave off a cold with less evidence and think we're being shrewd.

Building a prayer life is like putting scaffolding together. To change the spotlights in our church sanctuary, we have to pull out the scaffolding once a year. You start with a pile of metal pipes, braces, and wood planks on the floor. Then you begin to cobble it together. As you do so, you have to stand on what you've built to build it higher. It's a bottom-up process, and amazingly, it works. Before you know it, you're standing twenty feet up in the air changing lightbulbs!

The three components of a prayer scaffolding are: (1) prayer at intervals through the day, (2) weekly prayer with the community, and (3) seasonal celebrations. You've probably already begun to put yours together, but let's examine each component in more depth.

Prayer at Intervals Through the Day

For years I aimed to take a daily prayer time—at least a half hour, usually in the morning. That was my only frame of reference for daily prayer. I practice it still. But it's much easier now, since I started a practice called "fixed hour prayer": much shorter periods of prayer—as brief as two to three minutes—at intervals through the day. It took steady effort over many months to make it habit; but now that the habit is formed, it is easy and enormously help-ful. I only regret that it took me so long to try it.

I went through a period—all right, it was several decades!—when I thought my informal, conversational, and charismatic way of praying was far superior to the idea of "saying your prayers" with the help of a prayer book. I judged the prayer traditions of my childhood church, the Episcopal Church, to be sorely lack-ing in vitality—the way you pray when you've only got enough spiritual fuel in your tank to go through the motions.

How very wrong I was. How fitting that I made one of the most fruitful discoveries of my life when I purchased my first copy of *The Divine Hours: A Manual for Prayer* by Phyllis Tickle,[6] who happens to be a lay minister in the Episcopal Church of my upbringing. I shudder now that I almost didn't buy the book because the author was the religion editor for *Publishers Weekly*. What could a journalist teach me about prayer? Dear reader, hear my confession and pray the Lord have mercy on my soul!

As I learned from the book's introduction, the pattern of daily prayer at set intervals—roughly morning, noon, evening, and bedtime—is the baseline for daily prayer as it was practiced in the biblical era. In spite of decades of regular Bible reading, I had somehow missed this.

Daniel, an observant Jew who was taken captive in Babylon, kept a thrice-daily prayer practice: "Three times a day he got down on his knees and prayed, giving thanks to his God, just as he had done before" (Daniel 6:10). Though it is not indicated explicitly in the Gospels, Jesus likely maintained a similar practice as it was the custom in his day to say a prayer known as the *Shema* three times each day.[7]

The Psalms also bear ample witness to the practice. "Evening, morning and noon, / I cry out in distress, / and he hears my voice" (55:17). Or, "Seven times a day I praise you" (119:164).

During the New Testament era, bells sounded throughout the Roman Empire at fixed intervals: sunrise, nine a.m., noon, three p.m., and sundown. Devout Jews were found praying at these hours, including the earliest disciples of Jesus.

On the day of Pentecost, the church was gathered for prayer

---

6. Phyllis Tickle, *The Divine Hours: A Manual for Prayer* (New York: Doubleday, 2000).

7. *Shema* is the Hebrew word for "hear," which is the opening word of the closest thing Israel had to a creed: "Hear, O Israel: The Lord our God, the Lord is One. Love the Lord your God with all your heart and with all your soul and with all your strength" (Deuteronomy 6:4–5).

at nine a.m. when the Spirit was conferred (Acts 2:1, 15). The first recorded healing after the resurrection takes place as Peter and John walk to the temple "at the time of prayer—at three in the afternoon," the same hour that Jesus, weeks earlier, breathed his last prayer on the cross (Acts 3:1; Luke 23:44–46). Years later, Peter received a powerful vision on a rooftop in Joppa, where he was saying his noontime prayers (Acts 10:9).

Prayer at intervals through the day is part of the Jewish daily prayer tradition as well as the daily prayer tradition of Muslims. There are also echoes of fixed-hour prayer in the theistic recovery movement called Alcoholics Anonymous. In AA, participants are encouraged to pray first thing in the morning and last thing at night and to practice "checking in" with one's higher power throughout the day.[8]

My wife has been praying through the day for years, but without the aid of a prayer manual. Prayer throughout the day is the way she meets God in time.

Smaller Portions at More Frequent Intervals

You can eat one meal of 2,000 calories a day if you want to. But it's better to spread it out over three or four smaller meals.

I'm amazed at how many pastors I know who think it's very important to spend a lengthy time in prayer and scripture study once a day but find it extremely difficult to actually do it. And they are getting *paid* to pray! I don't think these are lazy pastors. I think it's more difficult to begin things the hard way.

Start with the breadth dimension of prayer (shorter segments

---

8. Specific set prayers are suggested for morning and evening as well as the "checking in" prayer commonly attributed to theologian Reinhold Niebuhr, the so-called Serenity Prayer: "God, grant me the serenity to accept the things I cannot change, courage to change the things I can, and the wisdom to know the difference."

at more frequent intervals) and then work on the depth dimension of prayer (a longer period once a day). You can't dig a deep hole without going wide first.

Once you establish the pattern of two or three or four shorter prayer segments throughout the day, you'll find it easier to use one of those times as a platform to go deeper in prayer.

In case you didn't notice, I just offered some advice: start wide before you try to go deep. It is general advice, though, which means it doesn't apply to everyone. My brother-in-law gets up at four-thirty a.m., goes to his La-Z-Boy chair, and does all four segments of the day's divine hours in one sitting.[9] Bill strings them all together at once and has a royal time. But if you've found it difficult to build a daily prayer habit by aiming for that once-a-day lengthy devotional time, aim for the pattern of short periods of prayer (say two to five minutes, tops) at more frequent intervals throughout the day.

> *Aim for the pattern of short periods of prayer (say five minutes, tops) at more frequent intervals throughout the day.*

I might just hang around a strange crowd, but I've found lots of people who think daily prayer means having one period of focused prayer that lasts thirty to sixty minutes every day, especially if they have learned a "daily prayer time method."[10] They attempt to go from sporadic, haphazard praying to a disciplined devotional time with no intervening steps. They feel mildly guilty that they can't do it. Some feel like failed followers.

---

9. The segments, by the way, are morning prayers, midday prayers, "vespers" (evening) prayer, and "compline" (bedtime) prayer.

10. One such method is the acronym ACTS: Adoration, Confession, Thanksgiving, Supplication. These four activities are presented as the four elements of a daily prayer time of thirty minutes to an hour, combined with Bible reading.

When they do manage to work in a half hour prayer time, they feel antsy for most of it. They assess each prayer time and find it wanting most times. It's like a gardener so eager to grow a healthy tomato plant that he plucks it out by the roots each day to see how it's doing. Not so good for the tomato plant.

Getting Started

Take an easy-does-it approach. Life's hard enough without *you* making it even more difficult!

Pick the right time to start this new habit. You have limited habit-formation energy reserves. You can't start multiple new habits at one time. You might not want to work on a new daily prayer habit when you're starting a new job or taking a new class—activities that draw down your habit-forming reserves.

Begin with your imagination. Picture yourself having a *short* time of prayer that you might actually look forward to. What location would make you look forward to it? What duration? What accompanying activities? What could you see yourself doing every day that you would look forward to doing? Bingo! Try that.

Leveraging Your Current Daily Habits First

To establish the practice of prayer at intervals through the day, start with one daily touch point for prayer and focus on working that into your routine until it is established. Leverage your current daily rhythms first, attaching prayer to something you already do habitually—like going to bed every night. Find a prayer book that works for you, place it on the nightstand next to your bed, and practice using it every night to form the habit of night prayers. This is often the easiest place to begin.

If you have a morning routine, like a cup of coffee, and you can see yourself having some morning prayers along with your cup of coffee, give that a try. If you boil a pot of water to make tea in the morning, you can say your morning prayers in that time, if time is short. Nothing is too easy not to count when it comes to prayer.

Once you have a daily prayer foothold established, add a second, then a third, even a fourth interval through the day. Measure progress in months, not days or weeks. Take weeks to establish a single time of daily prayer and more weeks (or months) to add a second interval and so on. Unless you have only a short time to live and are eager to pray at several intervals through the remaining days! Otherwise, avoid the go-for-broke approach. Easy does it, but steady as she goes.

Help From Prayer Aids

If you need help praying, use aids! If it helps, use it. You don't get extra credit for not using aid to prayer. I repeat: if you need help, use aids.

Remember, we're focusing on the habit formation aspect of daily prayer. Prayer aids are only aids if they make praying easier and more pleasant, if they help you form the daily habit of prayer. Prayer doesn't have to be easy or pleasurable to be good prayer. Jesus agonized in the garden as he prayed one of the most powerful prayers ever uttered: Not my will but yours be done. You will have your opportunity as well for agonizing prayer. But let's not start with the agony, shall we? So leverage your current pleasures, especially the ones that don't require your full attention. Guilt works by association, but so does pleasure. If you want to *enjoy* praying more, connect your praying to things you already enjoy.

For example, if you enjoy that mellow feeling after a time of vigorous exercise and you have already formed the habit of regular exercise, insert your prayer interval right after you finish exercising, while you're still feeling groovy.

People have been lighting candles to set aside times for prayer for millennia, because people like candles. Go with their collective wisdom if the practice appeals to you; spend a little extra on a candle that smells nice if that will help. Smells store memories. So if you want to convince yourself that prayer is pleasant, combine praying with a pleasant aroma.

Use background music, if that helps you to enjoy your prayers.

If you're still bothered by the idea that prayer aids are necessary in your case, think of them as training wheels that you can get rid of later if they get in the way of praying. Whatever you do, give your brain and your body the help they need to form a new habit.

By far the most helpful aid to prayer at intervals through the day is a prayer book containing set prayers for each of the prayer intervals. *The Book of Common Prayer* developed by the Anglican Communion is one such prayer book that many people enjoy, but I find it difficult to manage. It's a matter of personal preference.

For my money, you can't beat *The Divine Hours: A Manual for Prayer*.[11] The book comes in three volumes corresponding to the seasons with four periods of prayer covered each day, every day, for an entire year. Fumbling through pages or needing to know much about the liturgical calendar is kept to a minimum.

Each prayer segment (also called an "office") is written out in its entirety, covering roughly a page and a half. You can move quickly through the prayers and be done in a couple of minutes, or linger for much longer, as you like. The content of the prayers is drawn mainly from the Bible, with heavy use of the psalms.

I'm the sort of person who likes the idea of something before

---

11. Phyllis Tickle, *The Divine Hours: A Manual for Prayer* (Oxford: Oxford University Press, 2007).

liking the thing itself. I find that I tend to stick with the things I want to like when I like the idea of doing them long enough to acquire the actual taste for them, even when I run into little obstacles. Such was the case with using *The Divine Hours* as a manual for daily prayer. I hope many readers now like the idea of prayer at intervals through the day. It's a great place to start.

Your Resistant Brain

As happens when developing any new habit, be prepared to endure a little resistance from your brain. For all its ability to change, the brain is a conservative organ. Its primary job is to help you survive and maintain the habits that insure your survival.[12] When you try to introduce a new habit, your brain may protest a little. But you want to survive and thrive, so you will need to coax your brain into forming new habits.

As happens when developing any new habit, be prepared to endure a little resistance from your brain.

The resistance your brain puts up to new habit formation may appear impenetrable at first. Don't fall for it. What looks like a brick wall of resistance is actually only a thin sheet of paper. Note the resistance when it appears and laugh at it.

My brain tends to resist new prayer habits by assailing me with self-conscious or self-critical thoughts. Self-consciousness is the death of prayer; for me, it's the first obstacle to overcome in using new prayer forms. Ignore self-consciousness when it comes and eventually it will go away, though it may take awhile.

---

12. Andrew Newberg, MD, and Mark Robert Waldman, *How God Changes Your Brain* (New York: Ballantine, 2009), 175.

You may find this odd, but for the first two years I practiced the prayers of *The Divine Hours*, I frequently experienced annoyance when I prayed the Lord's Prayer—criticizing myself for rushing through it, wondering which version was better, examining whether or not I really meant it. I outlasted my brain's annoyance, and now I can't wait to get to the Lord's Prayer when I pray *The Divine Hours*.

Familiarity breeds contempt, but so does unfamiliarity. Both need to be overcome when we begin new prayer practices.

It doesn't help that our tribal nature often causes us to look down on the practices of those who are not part of "our group." When I began to use the liturgical prayers of my childhood tradition, it surfaced some lingering adolescent contempt I had indulged in when I broke with my childhood tradition to become an atheist and then later a nonliturgical "Jesus freak." I had to learn how to ignore this resistance in order to form this new prayer habit.

We tend to think of prayer as highly personal (which it is), and we tend to think of persons as isolated individuals (which they aren't); so using the prayers of others as our own personal prayer takes some getting used to. But getting used to it is well worth it.

Prayers that are entirely self-generated (the criteria for authenticity that least applies to Christian prayer) sometimes require enormous effort. Either that, or we lapse into saying the same things in only slightly different ways—feigned spontaneity. No wonder our prayers wear us out or bore us so quickly! But using the prayers of others as the springboard (not the full extent) of our praying brings a lovely ease to prayer. This eventually increases prayer's frequency and quality with much less effort than one would expect.

If you're up to it, try *The Divine Hours* or something like it for six weeks. Of the four daily prayer segments, just aim to use one or two a day during the six-week trial. If you can take a day or two to try all four in one day, go for it, but don't push it. The last thing you want to feel like is a failure. If after six weeks, you haven't gotten the bug—it feels more like a chore than anything else—put it down with a clear conscience. It may not be for you or may not be for you at this time in your life. Try something else.

It is possible to formulate your own prayer manual using the book of Psalms as your primary resource. One could, for example, pray an individual psalm (or portion of a longer psalm) two, three, or four times daily. Add a favorite set prayer (the Serenity Prayer, for example) or the Lord's Prayer, and you're in business. Do what works for you, and don't stick with what doesn't work for you. Prayer may require discipline, but it's not meant to be a form of punishment!

Weekly Prayer Intervals

If you want a daily prayer connection, then you'll need the other parts of the scaffolding to build it, including the weekly part. Genesis introduces the pattern of one day each week devoted to rest. Originally the rest was God's alone, but we are made in his image. So eventually Israel, representing the new human community, was invited to partake in the weekly Sabbath, marked by communal prayers.

The weekly worship gatherings remind us that God is a relational network, and if we want in with him we had better make room for others. For many, weekly worship with others is the first prayer rhythm established. But Christian prayer always involves an "I" praying with and to a "Thou," as part of a surrounding "we."

The weekly celebration provides the fodder for daily practice.

In the era before the printing press, people heard the Scriptures read on the Sabbath and memorized portions for use in their daily prayers. The stories and needs shared as the community gathered on the Sabbath would shape the daily prayers for the coming week. The weekly service of prayer reminded the participants that a powerful communal dimension enhanced their daily prayers.

It's possible to experience a vibrant daily connection with God without investing in a weekly pattern with others. It's possible to do a lot of things the hard way, but why work against nature—God's and your own?

You know a pattern is truly weekly when missing a week makes you feel slightly out of sync. That out-of-sync feeling, that subtle sense of being off balance, is evidence that a weekly prayer pattern has been set. If you don't feel out of sync missing something, it's probably because the pattern itself hasn't been established.

A week is admittedly an arbitrary way to mark time. Why not the British "fortnight" (two weeks)? I won't argue with you on that one. But I'll put my money on the deep wisdom of Genesis, echoed in the wisdom of many different cultures and traditions all of which seem to be saying the same thing: there's something about a weekly rhythm to time that seems to fit us because it fits God. Why fight it?

Seasonal Prayer Intervals

The prayer life of the people shaped by the Genesis understanding of God in time was further patterned around seasonal holidays. The festivals were festive because they were anticipated as breaks from routine labor. Extensive preparations were made so the celebrations could be enjoyed rather than simply endured.

Like any good party, these celebrations knit people together as a community. Three major holidays marked the year with minor feasts sprinkled in between.

There is a great power in annual special events that are variations on the same theme each year. My family has gone to the same vacation spot for thirty years in a row (and counting). Boring as the post office, you say? I'll grant you that those thirty vacations have not been high on the adventure index. But the fact that they have occurred at roughly the same time of year in the same physical surroundings means that my brain has formed some powerful neural pathways for vacation.

I have accumulated thirty years' worth of memories that are stimulated by simply being in the place where the memories were made at roughly the same time of year every year. When I drive down the dirt road lined with pines into the place we've gone many times before, the memories begin to surface, stored next to the place where my brain recognizes the scent of pine trees.[13]

There is a richness to experience that can only be conveyed by and measured in time, mysterious, priceless time.

There is a richness to experience that can only be conveyed by and measured in time, mysterious, priceless time.

Imagine that every day of your life were spent in a different location with different people doing different things. How would you remember anything? The brain is the great sifting and organizing system that draws meaning out of an otherwise stupefying stream of data. And to do its sifting and sorting job, the brain is looking for patterns. The one-off occurrences are great, but they stand

---

13. For the link between memory and smells, see Barry J. Gibb, *The Rough Guide to the Brain* (London: Rough Guides, Ltd., 2007), 53.

out only because the brain has anchored our experience in patterns. It is the quality of the patterns that makes for the quality of our lives.

Consider your favorite holiday.[14] What makes it your favorite? You will probably identify a *pattern* of activities and feelings, of sights and sounds and smells, of music and special foods or lighting, and of people doing things together. Last Christmas the thought hit me: *I'm fifty-seven! I won't have an unlimited supply of these things!* The Christmas season has become a way for me to mark and value time. As the psalmist said, "Teach us to number our days aright, / that we may gain a heart of wisdom" (Psalm 90:12).

The Holidays: Telling a Story through the Year

As we discussed in chapter 4, the brain makes sense of things by discerning, forming, and telling stories (a primary function of the left hemisphere of the brain). The seasonal festivals tell and retell a story through the year. The story comes in installments like the old serialized novels that were first released in a monthly magazine, chapter by chapter.

We often cruise through the holidays without pausing to remember that they are part of a yearlong story. So get your story straight to get the most out of the holidays. Here's the storyline told by the holidays of the church year:

At the height of darkness (in the Northern Hemisphere), we celebrate the birth of Jesus. It's no accident that darkness and light are a big part of Christmas celebrations. Epiphany follows Christmas twelve days later, when the church remembers the wise

---

14. If you don't have a favorite because you don't have a positive experience of any holidays, you may have the next best thing—a longing for one. Or like my friend, you may have started your own holiday; hers is called the "anti-holiday" and it has become the family favorite.

men from the East bearing gifts to Jesus in Bethlehem, introducing the theme of Jesus as the light of the world. The hostile interest of King Herod in the birth narratives reminds us that spiritual darkness does not retreat without a fight.

Come spring, we observe the season of Lent—a forty-day period that rehearses the time when Jesus went to the wilderness to prepare for his public ministry. Lent culminates in Holy Week, tracing the final days of Jesus' life on earth that led to his crucifixion. Easter is the celebration of the surprise ending that is a new beginning. The resurrection turns what started as a tragedy into a comedy, as God and good and light get the last laugh over Satan and evil and darkness. Life isn't just a blip on the screen of time. It's what triumphs over death.

Easter is followed ten days later by the celebration of the Ascension, at which time Jesus is installed as King in the heavenly realm, at God's right hand, to rule on our behalf and for our good. He is right next door, nearby, as close as our next breath. Forty days later we celebrate Pentecost, the day when the Father poured out the Spirit—the glorious love between the Father and the Son—on the church, in order to make this love available to all flesh. The story begins with flesh and blood (God-in-flesh appearing) and culminates in the Spirit poured out on all flesh and blood.

This leads us to Advent, the four Sundays before Christmas, when the church remembers the coming of Christ as a baby and eagerly awaits the renewal of all things at the end of this age and the beginning of the next.

To celebrate these events is to remind ourselves: God is making room for us in his story, and together with God, we are writing a new story for our own broken lives and for this broken world.

Building a Life of Prayer: The Long View

I have a friend who loves to say, "Anything worth doing is worth doing poorly."[15] In other words, anything that is intrinsically valuable, bordering on the essential, like eating or breathing or sleeping, is worth doing poorly rather than not at all.

Prayer is like that: it is worth doing poorly rather than not at all. Another way to say the same thing is this: when it comes to prayer, take the long view.

I'm a pastor, which doesn't exactly qualify me as a sex therapist. But I do have a little advice for engaged couples on their wedding night—especially when they've decided not to put the cart before the horse, let the reader understand, and are eagerly anticipating their first lovemaking. "You have an entire marriage ahead of you and plenty of time to become good at lovemaking. Don't put too much pressure on the wedding night. If you can enjoy the intimacy of nakedness and whatever happens after that, consider it a good start." This, and the advice to read Song of Songs, is about the extent of my lovemaking counsel.

When it comes to prayer, take the long view.

But it applies to prayer as well: take the long view. Your brain rewires by degrees, small degrees, over time. Easy does it. Start somewhere, establish a foothold, and make slow, steady progress.

It takes faith in the future to commit to the long view.

After graduating from high school, I thought I'd continue to run every day because I loved to run on the track and cross-country teams. I thought I loved running, that is. It turns out that I loved

---

15. Dave Mangan, the first Catholic charismatic. I know, I'm name dropping.

the competition, not the actual running. When the competition part was over, I wasn't motivated to do the running.

Life got pretty busy, and I didn't get around to establishing a regular exercise routine until much later in life, when I was firmly convinced that without regular exercise, I was not going to be able to handle the pressures of my job and the weight of my life.

When I first started to exercise at the gym, I looked forward to bulking up—you know, working on the old physique a little. But given my build and my age, without illegal steroids, bulking up is hard to do. You have to lift a lot of weights to bulk up. The guys my age who had muscular physiques spent a *lot* of time in the gym. I'd come in while they were working out and leave before they were done, no worse or bigger for the wear.

I had to do a little soul searching. Why was I exercising: to have some stuff to strut or to make it through the day?

Why do you want to pray: to strut your stuff or to make it through your day? I'll bet you're looking for help to make it through your day. Me too.

I've been exercising regularly for about eight years now, and I still ask myself, "How did I make it through my day without this? Bodies are built to move."

Prayer is like that too. Bodies are meant to pray their way through time.

EIGHT

In Depth: Dialing Down to Make Space for God

What happens when you close your eyes? As often as not, you become aware of the noise inside your head, what a fellow pastor calls his "steam of consciousness."[1] Have you ever tried to listen to the chatter inside your head? It can be unnerving—thoughts flitting to and fro, attaching themselves like burrs on your socks as you walk through a field. Sometimes the burrs are hard to remove.

Beneath many of the thoughts are feelings. The most powerful feelings that we experience from a neurological point of view are anger and fear in their various forms: frustration, tension, worry, irritation, annoyance, dread, anxiety, alarm.

What's happening in your brain when you experience anger or fear? The brain is forming and strengthening pathways made up of connections between nerve cells (neurons). Powerful chemicals, cortisol and norepinephrine, are released to reinforce these pathways.

Have you noticed that when someone speaks positive, affirming, or grateful words to you, it is fairly easy to forget the words,

---

1. Don Bromley, www.donbromleyblog.blogspot.com.

but when someone speaks angry or critical words they stick in your head for a long time? That's because the angry or critical words evoke anger or fear, and the neural pathways of anger and fear are more powerful than the pathways formed by pleasant feelings.

When we close our eyes to pray, we may become more aware of the noise inside our heads. No wonder we do our business quickly, open our eyes back up, and try to do something—anything—that will distract us from the noise.

Perhaps this is why our brains put up a fuss when we try to pray, why they turn into snarky little children responding to a simple request whining, "Do I *have* to?" (I'm not the only one this happens to, right?)

So Relax, Already!

There's something you can do to help: add a relaxation component to your regular prayers. This will do a few things: over time, it will improve the experience of your prayers; it may allow you to experience new depths of prayer; and it will provide your brain a powerful incentive to pray more often, because it feels better to pray this way.

Many kinds of praying can have a calming effect. Prayers of petition can calm us by assuring us of God's help in times of trouble. Praying charismatically, through active means like dancing, rhythmic clapping, or praying in tongues, can have a calming effect. But the disciplines of contemplative prayer—silence, solitude, meditative prayer, reflecting on scripture, and so on—are especially designed to be calming.[2] We can calm ourselves through contemplative prayer.

---

2. Of course, nothing is as simple as it seems; contemplative prayer may also uncover deep pain or mediate an experience of God that produces a sense of awestruck fear, but this is more the exception than the rule.

Psalm 131 models this for us:

> *My heart is not proud, O Lord,*
>   *my eyes are not haughty;*
> *I do not concern myself with great matters*
>   *or things too wonderful for me.*
> *But I have stilled and quieted my soul;*
>   *like a weaned child with its mother,*
>   *like a weaned child is my soul within me.*
> *O Israel, put your hope in the Lord*
>   *both now and forevermore.*

We are made to think big thoughts and to make big plans—to set high goals and strain to achieve them. But we often try to do this alone from God. Alone from God, we naturally strive to be up to the challenge before us, whatever it is. Sometimes we lose our sense of proportion. We are strong! We are mighty! We are powerful! Except when we're not. When we fall into this trap, we need to extract ourselves by regaining a sense of proportion, by remembering our human limitations.

That's especially when we need to "still and quiet" ourselves, as the psalm says. Just as a child who has been nursing at his mother's breast eventually has to be weaned and learn to calm himself down without nursing—not without his mother, but in nearness to his mother—we learn to calm ourselves in the presence of God.

This calming makes it possible for us to anticipate the future with God ("hope in the Lord") rather than without God, the prideful default setting of our species.

Psalm 131, in other words, is a picture of contemplative prayer. And there is a part for us to play in such praying: learning to still and quiet ourselves.

Be Still and Know

The discipline of stillness[3] and its corollary, silence,[4] is commended in Scripture in many different places and forms.

- "When you are on your beds, / search your hearts and be silent" (Psalm 4:4).
- "He leads me beside quiet waters, / he restores my soul" (Psalm 23:2–3).
- "Be still, and know that I am God" (Psalm 46:10).
- "In quietness and trust is your strength" (Isaiah 30:15).
- "The LORD is in his holy temple; / let all the earth be silent before him" (Habakkuk 2:20).
- "When he opened the seventh seal, there was silence in heaven for about half an hour" (Revelation 8:1).

Stillness is widely practiced as a spiritual discipline. As Dallas Willard points out in his excellent book, *The Spirit of the Disciplines*, the spiritual disciplines are really bodily disciplines, analogous to the rhythms that sustain biological life, such as breathing and eating.[5] We are need-based units who require energy from outside of ourselves to sustain our own life. Breathing brings oxygen from the air into our bodies; eating brings energy from food into our bodies. We form habits to ensure that we have

---

3. *Still,* adj. 1. remaining in place or at rest; motionless; stationary; *to stand still.* 2. free from sound or noise, as a place, persons, etc.: silent: *to keep still about a matter* 3. subdued or low in sound; hushed: *a still, small voice.* 4. free from turbulence or commotion; peaceful; tranquil; calm; the still air. From *The Random House Dictionary of the English Language* (New York: Random House, 1983).

4. Stillness has to do with motion, while silence has to do with sound—two expressions of the same underlying phenomenon.

5. Dallas Willard, *The Spirit of the Disciplines* (New York: HarperOne, 1990), 57–60, 67–68.

means to receive from beyond ourselves what we lack within ourselves in order to sustain ourselves. The spiritual disciplines do the same for our embodied life in the Spirit: they train our bodies to receive life and refreshment from God.

Anthony Bloom is a compelling witness to the power of stillness precisely because he was an activist—a physician during World War II, who later became an Orthodox bishop. In his helpful book *Beginning to Pray*, Bloom describes the nature of the stillness that constitutes the discipline of stillness.[6] He likens the spiritual discipline of stillness to the stillness of a bird watcher who gets up early in the morning to sight a rare bird known to inhabit a particular place in a forest. The bird watcher sits quietly on a log and keeps his body as still as possible so as not to frighten away any birds . . . and waits—alert, but calm and quiet. He realizes that he can't make the bird appear; he simply wants to be in a position to see the bird if it does. The practiced bird watcher learns to appreciate the stillness as well as the bird.

I discovered Anthony Bloom's book on prayer in my father's bookcase when cleaning out his apartment after his death. We had provided hospice care in our home during his illness and I was tired, physically and spiritually. Some think that a mild depression can serve as the body's way of slowing us down; it enforces a kind of withdrawal that can be restorative if it doesn't go overboard, much like a bear going into hibernation. I was going into hibernation.

My father was a bird watcher, something I didn't pay much attention to until he died. But to preserve fond memories of my father, I purchased a bird feeder and placed it outside of my office window near the corner I use for prayer. This particular bird feeder attaches right to the window, to draw the birds up close.

---

6. Anthony Bloom, *Beginning to Pray* (New York: Paulist Press, 1970), 91–92.

When you set up a new bird feeder, the birds don't discover it instantly. It can take days before you spot your first bird feeding there. I would have liked my gratification sooner rather than later, but the birds weren't cooperating.

One morning, inspired by Bloom's description of silence, I sat at the little prayer corner in my office and practiced a meditation on Psalm 46:10: "Be still, and know that I am God." It's a simple method that allows you to memorize a verse as you ponder it. Read the verse over a few times, then start with the first word, and build from there as follows: *Be . . . Be still . . . Be still, and . . . Be still, and know . . .* At the precise moment in the meditation when I got to the final word—*Be still and know that I am God*—wouldn't you know it, my first bird, a blue jay—my dad's favorite bird—landed on the bird feeder on the outside of my office window. It was a blessed moment.

We Are Stillness Deprived

Modern life has advantages for those not living in abject poverty: clean drinking water, antibiotics to cure life-threatening infections, glasses (I'd be draft deferrable without mine), and ready access to food. But it comes at a cost: a way of living that doesn't lend itself to restorative periods of stillness, silence, and solitude.

Most of us practice a form of stillness that drains rather than replenishes us, that busies rather than calms the brain: watching television or playing video games. By age seventy, the average person will have spent seven to ten years of his or her life watching televsion.[7] Children watch about three hours of television a day, on

---

7. Miriam E. Bar-on, MD, "Children, Adolescents, and Television," *Pediatrics*, vol. 107, no. 2 (February 2001).

average, which does not include time spent playing video games.[8]
Watching television stimulates the brain by providing a series of
shifting images; this seems to lead to attention difficulties, especially in young children.[9] This replaces more refreshing forms of
relaxation like talking to friends or enjoying a sunset, reading, or
knitting. Forms of relaxation from a bygone era, like hunting and
fishing, entail long hours outdoors being relatively quiet and waiting
for something to happen, or walking through woods and fields.

The word *meditate* first appears in the Bible when Isaac "went
out to the field one evening to meditate, and as he looked up,
he saw camels approaching" (Genesis 24:63). It was a poignant
scene. Isaac had lost his mother, Sarah, who favored him, and he
was about to lose his father, Abraham. Isaac was out in the fields
meditating. Then along came his father's servant, bringing the
beautiful Rebekah, who was to become his wife.

What was Isaac in need of that drew him out to the field one
evening to meditate?

The text doesn't specify, but we can imagine that he needed
to relax. He needed to cease from his other activity—mental and
otherwise—and rest, a need that is central to what it means for us
to be in the "image of God," who ceased from his creative activity
to rest on the seventh day (Genesis 2:2).

Breathe—In and Out

The key to relaxation goes back to the first picture in the Bible of
a human being in close proximity to God: "Then the Lord God
fashioned the human, humus from the soil, and blew into his

---

8. Ibid.
9. Dimitri A. Kristakis et al., "Early Television Exposure and Subsequent Attentional
   Problems in Children," *Pediatrics* 113 (2004): 708–713.

nostrils the breath of life, and the human became a living creature" (Genesis 2:7 ALTER).

The simplest way to relax is to do as Adam did: take a deep
breath—in and out.[10]

While we think of breathing as natural, what we call "natural" is actually quite spiritual, since nature comes from God. The
word for breath in Hebrew (*ruah*) and in Greek (*pneuma*)—the
language of the Old Testament and the New Testament respec-
tively—also means "spirit." That's saying something about the
importance of breath.

I understand when some of my pastor colleagues get nervous about combining prayer with relaxation methods. They
want to insist (rightly) that Christian prayer involves God and
is more than this or that method. But prayer is also a human
activity that involves various actions that could be described as
methods.

When a pastor says, "Let's close our eyes and bow our heads
and pray," he is advocating the use of a particular prayer technique.
When we pray, prayer is happening in and with our bodies, and
there are certain things we do with our bodies in order to pray.
There's nothing wrong with that. In fact, we can't pray without
doing certain things with our bodies. Relaxing by breathing is
also something we can do with our bodies to pray.

The particular kind of breathing that relaxes us is deep
breathing: slowly and gently filling our lungs with air and slowly
and gently exhaling. In with the fresh air, out with the stale air.

Psalms is the prayer book of the Bible. More accurately, it
is the Bible's hymnal because the psalms were meant to be sung.

---

10. In their book *How God Changes Your Brain* (New York: Ballantine, 2009), 182–83,
Dr. Andrew Newberg and Mark Robert Waldman describe the fastest way to
relax—by yawning. Think of Adam yawning after waking up in the Garden for the
very first time.

Hence the psalms include editorial insertions like "to the tune of" and "selah," which may mean "pause."

Singing aloud is a form of deep breathing. Any good voice coach will tell you: sing from the diaphragm, not the throat—meaning, pull a good load of air into your lungs by raising your belly to make room, then push with your abdominal muscles, to release as much of the air in your lungs as possible. Deep breathing is one of the reasons it can be so fun to sing—it's relaxing!

So rhythmic deep breathing is an effective way to relax. This will slow down your other thoughts and make your mind more alert, something that is good for prayer.[11]

Here's How to Do It

When you pray, begin by taking some deep breaths. Inhale through your nose and exhale through your mouth to the count of five. Inhale—one, two, three, four, five; exhale—one, two, three, four, five. Depending on your need to relax, take deep breaths in sets of four: four, eight, twelve, or sixteen. To count without having to strain your brain, simply touch your thumb to your four fingers in sequence. Sixteen breaths is four hands' worth.

It may not always be possible, but it's preferable to breathe through your nose, like Adam's first breath. This does a few things: it slows your breathing down; it's better at straining out dust and small bugs (a real plus!); and it "increases the release of nitric oxide in your body and this is good for your lungs and circulatory system."[12]

Pay attention to your breathing when you are taking deep

---

11. "Be clear minded and self-controlled so that you can pray." (1 Peter 4:7)

12. Andrew Newberg, MD, and Mark Robert Waldman, *How God Changes Your Brain: Breakthrough Findings from a Leading Neuroscientist* (New York: Ballantine, 2009), 180.

breaths to relax. You'll notice that the air is cooler when you inhale and warmer when you exhale.[13] And like the choir director told you, pay attention to "breathing from the midsection." Feel your abdomen rise first and then your chest as you inhale. The mere act of paying attention to your breathing shifts your attention away from your busy thoughts to your less busy body. This is precisely the kind of break that your brain needs most.

Try it right now, if you're the try-it-now type: take sixteen deep breaths, counting by touching the four fingers of your hand to your thumb; in through the nose—one, two, three, four, five; and out through the nose—one, two, three, four, five.

If you actually practiced that little exercise, it probably took about two and a half minutes. And you feel more relaxed as a result. Surprisingly, you may also feel more alert, not sleepier—unless you were ready to sleep in the first place. Congratulations: you have taken a small step forward in learning to "still and quiet" yourself and in clearing your mind to pray. You can do it.

Help Yourself *Want* to Pray More Often

Here's a secret to help you pray more often: pick a form of set prayers at intervals through the day and begin by taking a minute or two to simply relax with some deep breathing. Then begin the prayers for the interval. When you come to the Lord's Prayer, about two-thirds of the way through each prayer period (called an "office" because prayer is the divine "work"), tie this prayer to another round of deep breathing.

Go ahead, try it right now.

---

13. Adding incense also naturally slows down our breathing, as smelling requires a more thoughtful breathing. For a great little essay on smell, see Diane Ackerman, *A Natural History of the Senses* (New York: Vintage Books, 1995), 3–63.

I've divided the Lord's Prayer into five deep breaths: the inhale is in regular font; the exhale is in *italics*.

> Our Father in heaven,
> *hallowed be your name,*
> your kingdom come,
> your will be done
>   *on earth as it is in heaven.*
> Give us today our daily bread.
> *Forgive us our debts,*
>   *as we also have forgiven our debtors.*
> And lead us not into temptation,
> *but deliver us from the evil one.*
> [For yours is the kingdom and the power and the glory
>   forever. *Amen.*]

Once you practice this a few times, you will be less self-conscious about the breathing. The slow breathing will slow you down and help you to focus on this powerful prayer.

But here's the secret part: your brain will offer less resistance to the idea of praying at intervals through the day, because your brain will learn that prayer is relaxing—that it *feels good.*

Pray the Jesus Prayer Combined with Breathing

In chapters 1 and 3, I mentioned the Jesus Prayer. This prayer from the Eastern Orthodox tradition combines two biblical phrases, "Lord Jesus Christ, son of the living God"[14] and "have mercy on

---

14. From Peter's confession, "You are the Christ, the Son of the living God" in Matthew 16:16.

me, a sinner."[15] The Orthodox practice ties the prayer to breathing: "Lord Jesus Christ, son of the living God [on the inhale] have mercy on me, a sinner [on the exhale]." The phrases can be simplified, as in, "Lord Jesus, Son of God, have mercy on me."

You can decide to repeat the prayer a certain number of times, using a string of "prayer beads" to count without having to pay attention to the numbers. This is the equivalent of counting by touching the fingers of the hand in sequence with your thumb. The prayer beads work better for tracking lengthier periods of using the prayer, because there are more beads on the string than fingers on your hands. (Who says you'll never use math in real life?)

Why would we want to keep track of the number of times we repeat the Jesus Prayer? Prayer beads were invented before the wristwatch or the egg timer, but they accomplish the same thing. If you are particularly stressed, you may want to use the Jesus Prayer for a longer period before you move on to other ways of praying, so you say to yourself, "I'll do three rounds of the Jesus Prayer rather than two."

Some may object to this practice on the grounds that praying a simple prayer like this over and over amounts to something forbidden by Jesus when he said, "And when you pray, do not keep on babbling like pagans, for they think they will be heard because of their many words" (Matthew 6:7).

Jesus was forbidding a pagan approach to prayer that involved what other translations call either "vain repetitions" or perhaps "babbling." In the case of the pagan practice of "vain repetitions," the repetitions were made *so that* the god or goddess might hear

---

15. From the parable of the Pharisee and the tax collector, who prayed, "God, have mercy on me, a sinner" (Luke 18:13).

what is being said—much as my wife occasionally repeats things to me because I'm not a very good listener. This is not the purpose of praying the Jesus Prayer.

The purpose of praying the Jesus Prayer is to focus attention on Jesus, the friend of sinners, and to relax so that our minds are more alert for prayer. There are many other examples of repetitive prayers throughout the Bible (see, for example, the use of "his love endures forever" as a refrain in Psalm 136, or the use of the threefold "holy, holy, holy" throughout the Bible).

The Eastern Orthodox recommend the Jesus Prayer as a way to "pray without ceasing" (1 Thessalonians 5:17 NASB). By tying the prayer to one's breathing, it is possible to continue the prayer throughout the day while doing other things. The mind is able to adapt and focus on other things while also praying the Jesus Prayer. The prayer becomes a way for your heart to stay "tuned in" to Jesus while you go about your daily activities. It sounds rather strange, I know, but it works.

On a lark, I tried doing it for an entire day—Thanksgiving, of all days, when we had several guests over. At first I thought this might not be a good idea. Could I be a good host while keeping the Jesus Prayer going under the surface of my thoughts while I interacted normally with everyone else? But curiosity got the better of me—it seemed possible to do, so I persisted.

When the guests left, my wife, Nancy, said, "I appreciated how extra helpful and attentive you were today with all the people over. It really helped."

I was? How was that possible? I was praying the Jesus Prayer the whole time.

This prayer seemed to induce a form of mental awareness that was not unlike a calm and meditative period of silence, one of those blessed times when the mind isn't running wild with intrusive thoughts. Throughout the day it felt a little like I was daydreaming, except that I was able to pay attention to what was going on around me. At any rate, the effect is remarkably calming.

Relaxation Allows You to Go Deeper

Relaxation is a reasonable end in itself. But relaxation can also become a means to a different end: it can allow us to go deeper into prayer. By "going deeper," I mean that it can allow us to attend to God better, it can promote a deeper sense of connection with God, and it can open our minds and hearts to recognize and respond to God's presence.

I learned this from John Wimber.[16] Wimber was an interesting guy. Before becoming a pastor, he was the manager-producer of the Righteous Brothers. Wimber was a jazz musician who could play the piano for hours at a time. I suspect it helped him to relax; and the relaxing, I also suspect, helped him to open his heart to God. In other words, it was for him, a way to pray, or at least it helped him to pray.[17]

John Wimber is known primarily for helping evangelical Christians who were not part of the Pentecostal movement to learn how to receive gifts of the Spirit to do works of the kingdom like healing the sick. Wimber departed from the conventional practice of charismatic and Pentecostal Christians in several respects, not least of which is his insistence that in order to "listen" to the Spirit's promptings, it is important to "dial down" rather "dial

---

16. John Wimber was a prominent leader in the Vineyard movement, which led to an association of churches called Vineyard: a Community of Churches, of which my church, the Vineyard Church of Ann Arbor, is a part.

17. This is based on personal conversation with Kevin Springer, a friend of mine who worked closely with John Wimber for several years.

up." By this he meant several things—but chief among them is the need to still and quiet the soul by relaxing, rather than "revving up" by such things as energetic verbal prayer.

Understand the Dynamics of "Going Deeper"

Language like "going deeper" can frustrate me. It sounds like a wine connoisseur describing a particular wine as "bold and fruity, but with a crisp, clean finish." Come on! What does the wine taste like, already?

The fact is, we only have a few English words designed to describe taste: *salty, sour, sweet, bitter.* We don't have many words designed to describe connection with the divine either.

Prayer involves experiences that are not easy to translate into concrete images. It's not hot or cold, blue or green, hard or soft. We can speak of the outwardly physical aspects of the praying person (e.g., kneeling, eyes closed, hands raised), but what's going on in the inwardly physical aspects of the praying person— there in his or her brain, or wherever it is that something is happening? That's another matter entirely. We can only use metaphors—like "going deeper"—to form correspondences that infer what's going on.

> *Prayer involves experiences that are not easy to translate into concrete images.*

Given the limits of language, let me try to be more specific about what I mean by the phrase "going deeper" in prayer.

Thoughts Slow Down

When going deeper, the ordinary cascade of thought that occupies the conscious mind seems to slow down. The barrage of thoughts that constitute waking awareness don't cease, but they do seem to either slow down or demand less attention, in much the same way that the sound of voices around the swimming pool are muted when you put your head underwater.

To switch metaphors, think of it like the common cinematic technique in which the camera focuses on an object in the foreground that comes into clear focus while the background objects blur. "Going deeper" involves a shift like that: the ordinary chatter in your head moves from the clearly focused foreground to the blurry background.

This shift allows a person to become more aware of other things going on in the brain.

Previously Subtle Phenomena Are Noticed

A friend who runs the catering business of a high-end delicatessen in Ann Arbor brought me a small bar of chocolate that cost twelve dollars. He told me the story of the chocolate bar, tracing key ingredients from a field in Guatemala to a kitchen in Kansas City where the ingredients were mixed together, then sent straight to the Ann Arbor delicatessen before arriving in my hands.

Because of my friend's description of the chocolate bar and its unusual cost, my brain was focused in an extraordinary way on the chocolate in my mouth. I didn't wolf it down like a Hershey's Kiss while my mind focused on something else. No, I paid close attention to the taste, smell, and texture of the chocolate in my mouth and the distinction between the chocolate taste and the crunchy little bits of vanilla. I was savoring the chocolate bar.

When our ordinary thoughts slow down or recede into the background of our attention, our brains are able to savor other things—to notice subtleties that were previously unnoticed.

Occasionally, in this state of awareness, we sense (hear, see, smell, taste, feel) things that we might not otherwise. A phrase like "Be still, and know that I am God" (Psalm 46:10) suggests that God likes to make himself known in this space.

Imagine a crowded room with voices engaged in multiple conversations. In the middle of the room, someone is speaking to you in a quiet voice that can't be heard above the din. But then slowly, the other conversations fade into the background as the people doing the talking move to the edge of the room. Eventually you hear the voice of the person speaking to you.

The prophet Isaiah said of God, "He will not shout or cry out, / or raise his voice in the streets. / A bruised reed he will not break, / and a smoldering wick he will not snuff out" (Isaiah 42:2–3). Some of the things that we need to hear can only be heard quietly.

Our Sense of a Separated Self Blurs

A powerful hormone is released during sexual intercourse that produces a sense of unity or bonding with the beloved. This is the same hormone released in a mother who has given birth to an infant, and in lesser quantities to a father who witnesses the birth. It's also released in mother and infant during nursing.[18]

To make our way in the world, we need to have a sense of self that is separate from other people and things. So parents have to learn to let go of their children, and children have to leave their father and mother in order to cleave to another to form a new family or to otherwise pursue their life's task.

But we also need a sense of connection with others—to feel our sameness with them and not simply our differences: we need

---

18. Pierce J. Howard, PhD, *The Owner's Manual for The Brain: Everyday Applications from Mind-Brain Research* (Austin, TX: Bard Press, 2006), 760.

leaving and cleaving, a sense of separateness and a sense of same-ness. This dynamic tension or paradox is central to the Christian vision of God as a Trinity of persons: three distinct persons—Father, Son, Holy Spirit—sharing one divine substance.

There's a great deal in the modern world that reinforces the sense of the separated self: wearing distinct clothing, driving alone in separate vehicles, listening to personally designed playlists on our iPods—there's so much in our daily lives to reinforce our separateness. We need to have ways of feeling our connectedness.

This is what can happen in prayer of the contemplative variety. In chapter 2, we discussed "unitive experiences" and their underlying neurology, described by the research of Drs. Andrew Newberg and Eugene D'Aquili. As the attention portion of the brain focuses intently on one thing, the "orientation association area" located in the parietal lobe of the brain, just above and behind the ear, receives less stimulation. This portion of the brain is called the orientation association area because it orients us with respect to our surroundings. It helps define the self as separate from other things. The reduced activity in this portion of the brain corresponds to a sense of blurring between the self and one's surroundings.

Depending on what the person meditating is focused on, he or she may feel connected with others, with God, or with his or her surroundings. It is a powerfully pleasant experience and it seems to have a transformative effect on those who practice it regularly.

Relaxation Brings Us Back for More

We're too wound up. We need help relaxing in ways that aren't destructive to ourselves and to others. And we need to find ways to relax when we pray, if for no other reason than that it will help us to pray more.

That's exactly what I found happening to me when I began to engage in prayer practices that had the effect of inducing a relaxation response. I didn't set out to relax. I simply set out to pray beyond ways that had become a little stale and required more effort than I could muster. I had no idea what I was missing.

As a result of stumbling somewhat blindly into these practices, I found myself returning to prayer more frequently through the day and for more extended periods of time almost daily. And all this seemed to be happening with less effort (what I thought of as "discipline") than ever before.

Like marriage, or any other committed relationship for that matter, there's enough about prayer that is difficult. We have these lives to live, and it takes so much effort to live them. Given our human frailty, we need to pay attention to things that bring us back for more.

NINE

Eyes Open: With Jesus in the Outdoor Cathedral

A typical day in a typical life: You wake up, go through your morning routine, and hop into the car for a twenty-minute commute. Most of the way, you're either fumbling for something on the radio or planning for your workday. (By now, you know better than to fiddle with your phone.) You park the car and walk quickly to your workplace, preoccupied with thoughts of the day ahead. You enter a nondescript building, find your fluorescent-lit cubicle, turn on your computer, and get down to business—phone calls, e-mail, meetings, more phone calls. Then it's back out to the car and the commute through heavy traffic. You're back in time for dinner, to help the kids with their homework, read the paper, squeeze in a favorite television show, catch up on some personal e-mails, and go to bed. Repeat.

Every day, this routine takes place on a planet that is throbbing with life—a slowly shifting platform of varied topography, hills and mountains, flatlands, deserts, forests, or whatever else your portion of the planet is featuring during this particular epoch. If you could rise to a wide enough angle, you'd see a continental landscape surrounded by oceans—another world within a world that few of us have time, inclination, or resources to explore.

We're in a cathedral, and it's a mystical wonderland not built by human hands.

All of this occurs beneath a canopy of varied hues—mottled grays or brilliant blues or darkness pierced by points of sparkling light, day and night presided over by alternating orbs of yellow and white. It's all swept new, this place, by wind and mysterious visitations of water in dispersed droplets.

We're in a cathedral, and it's a mystical wonderland not built by human hands. The rain on our faces is holy water from a divine aspergillum, the smells, incense from a swinging censer, and the sounds are the voices of a terrestrial choir.

Your Brain on Nature

The brain craves the outdoors so long as it can find shelter from the storm and heat and cold as needed. The mystically wired brain especially craves the outdoors—the brain in search of God and beauty and something of interest.

Confine a man in a prison cell, and he'll be more likely to get out sooner and not return if he has a window looking out into the cathedral of nature. A patient recovering from surgery in a hospital room with a view of the outdoor cathedral will heal faster.[1]

What the old wisdom has known for millennia—that the earth

---

1. Howard Frumpkin, MD, PhD, "Beyond Toxicity: Human Health and the Natural Environment," *American Journal of Preventive Medicine*, 2001; 20(3): 236–37.

is a temple, a sacred place—the new wisdom of science confirms in its own way. It's even been given a name: biophilia, the love of nature.[2]

We have favorite places in this outdoor cathedral that seem to be wired into the brain: running water (which tends to be cleaner) and places offering shelter from the elements and enemies, and trees and bushes and flowering plants where food might be found.[3]

And the brain is a sucker for a good view. One in five golfers never break 100.[4] I've never broken 120, even when I use the "Bill Clinton rules."[5] So why do I keep at it? Because of the view!

Those who have the resources often use them to purchase a home near the edge of a forest overlooking a field of green. Like a golf course. The brain releases pleasure at that particular sight, perhaps because our ancestors learned that it was a landscape that gave them the best chance of survival.[6]

Your brain is wired to respond to nature with an alert curiosity.

Your brain is wired to respond to nature with an alert curiosity—to scan for treasure, for blessings, for clues to what may be ahead or behind or nearby, lurking as threats or offering some advantage to your well being. If you're bored, it may be a sign that your mystical wiring wants you to go outdoors where things are more interesting.

---

2. E. O. Wilson, *Biophilia: The Human Bond with Other Species* (Cambridge: Harvard University Press, 1984).

3. Frumpkin, "Beyond Toxicity," 236–37.

4. Mike Adams, Mike Corcoran, with T. J. Thomas, *Break 100: From Hacker to Golfer in Just Ninety Days* (New York: HarperCollins, 1998), 2.

5. See article at Newsmax.com quoting Tiger Woods' description of President Clinton's "flexible scoring system," . . . archive.newsmax.com/archives/ic/2006/5/31/175721.shtml.

6. Frumpkin, "Beyond Toxicity," 236–37.

Nature: An Acquired Taste
for Those Who Don't Get Out Enough

Parents of children who spend a lot of time indoors (as most children do now) know the feeling. You've planned and saved for a family vacation in order to provide your children with an enriching experience. You are arriving at your destination—Yosemite National Park, perhaps, or the Grand Tetons. "This is some gorgeous scenery!" you say. Then, "Kids, look outside!"

The kids offer an obligatory glance and say, "Nice!" before putting their heads back into the latest digital device or busying their thumbs with the latest video game.

I can remember driving with my parents into yet another national park on a vacation that seemed to last forever. They kept urging me to look outside, but all I could see from my perch in the backseat was a hypnotizing sequence of telephone poles and electric wire. Their view was better.

It's not the kids' fault; it's the fault of the brain's adaptive strategy. We and our children spend an increasing amount of time inside buildings. Fewer of us go fishing or hunting, and attendance in our national parks is on the decline. School hours are lengthening, homework is increasing, and summer vacations are packed with organized activities, many of them indoors.[7]

All of this time indoors is very uninteresting to the human brain, so it scans for indoor points of interest. Curiosity is part of the learning capacity that gives human beings a survival advantage, so the brain will seek out venues to exercise it.

In inside landscapes, the most interesting spaces are video screens, especially of the high-definition variety. I recently watched the BBC documentary *Planet Earth* on my son's large plasma

---

7. Richard Louv, *Last Child in the Woods* (Chapel Hill: Algonquin Books, 2008) 34–37.

screen television. *Wow*, I thought, *this is more beautiful than the real planet Earth!*

The flashing images quickly capture the brain's attention, then, over time, lull them into a kind of stupor that makes it more difficult to disengage. Many video games are carefully programmed to provide the brain with randomized rewards—like slot machines—that release a surge of dopamine, the pleasure chemical, to keep kids coming back for more.[8] Dopamine makes a dope of many of us.

Nature, by comparison, offers a deeper and slower pleasure to the brain. And much of the fascination of nature is obscured in urban and suburban landscapes by roads, buildings, advertising, and artificial lighting. The interesting stuff, in other words, is hidden from view. Without multiple exposures, the brain doesn't learn how fascinating nature can be.

Nature and the Mystically Wired Jesus

What does nature have to do with prayer, you may ask? Simply this: many of us don't pray enough because we don't get outdoors enough. The kind of curiosity and calming and reflective meditation that can happen with our mystically wired brain often happens best in the outdoor cathedral of prayer.

Jesus did most of his praying outdoors. Even when he prayed in the temple courts, he was praying in a kind of outdoor mall setting, with a clear view of the sky and the sound of sheep and goats and birds.

But there's a deeper significance to fact that Jesus did his

---

8. For a description of the addictive power of randomized rewards, see the discussion of slot machines and dopamine in Jonah Lehrer, *How We Decide* (New York: Houghton Mifflin, 2009), 58–62.

praying outdoors. While we refer to the outdoors as nature, Jesus and his people knew it only as creation. The Hebrews didn't use the term *nature*, and there was no distinction between the natural and supernatural; what we call "nature" they called "creation," a work of God through and through.

Furthermore, the entire creation or cosmos was viewed as a temple.[9] The seven days of creation in the book of Genesis can be viewed as the inauguration of the world as a temple, much like the inauguration of the tabernacle in Exodus 40, which culminates in the glory of the Lord taking up residence in the tabernacle. On the seventh day of creation, God took up residence in the world; having set up the functions of the world in the first six days, his presence came to rest there on the seventh day.

Jesus prayed outdoors because he saw the world as a temple filled with the glory of God.

Prayer in the River

The first time we discover Jesus praying in the Gospels, he is praying in a river. "When all the people were being baptized, Jesus was baptized too. And as he was praying, heaven was opened and the Holy Spirit descended on him in bodily form like a dove. And a voice came from heaven: 'You are my Son, whom I love; with you I am well pleased'" (Luke 3:21–22).

The outdoor location is not incidental to his experience of God in prayer, is it? Jesus is kneeling in running water, under an open sky, with (as Matthew's account adds) "the Spirit of God descending like a dove and lighting on him" (Matthew 3:16). After that, do you think Jesus could ever look at a dove without

---

9. For a full exposition of this reading of Genesis 1, see John H. Dalton, *The Lost World of Genesis One: Ancient Cosmology and the Origins Debate* (Downers Grove, IL: IVP Academic, 2009).

feeling God's favor? Or bathe in a river without feeling God's presence? Or look at the sky as if nothing were there?

From that day forward, we find Jesus praying in the outdoor cathedral.

Morning Prayer in a Solitary Place

"Very early in the morning, while it was still dark, Jesus got up, left the house and went off to a solitary place, where he prayed" (Mark 1:35). Did Jesus get up while it was still dark because he wanted to pray with the dawn as his backdrop—the morning star and the rising sun?

My daughter-in-law rises early, leaves the three kids with her sleeping husband, and prays and walks outside. When it's too cold out, she turns on the Sunrise Earth channel and says her morning prayers.

There are times when your brain would like you to go outdoors, find a solitary place, and pray.

Prayers on a Mountainside

On another occasion, Jesus was distressed. His cousin John had been murdered. He wanted to get away to mourn, but work wouldn't let him. So he took care of business and then he went to pray, again, in the outdoor cathedral: "Immediately Jesus made his disciples get into the boat and go on ahead of him to Bethsaida, while he dismissed the crowd. After leaving them, he went up on a mountainside to pray" (Mark 6:45–46).

Yet another example: "About eight days after Jesus said this, he took Peter, John and James with him and went up onto a mountain to pray. As he was praying, the appearance of his face changed, and his clothes became as bright as a flash of lightning. . . . While he was speaking, a cloud appeared and enveloped them, and they were afraid as they entered the cloud. A voice came from the cloud, saying, 'This is my Son, whom I have chosen; listen to him'" (Luke 9:28–29, 34–35).

If the Gnostics are right, and this world is no more significant than the shell of a peanut, and the real action has nothing to do with creation or matter, then the setting for prayer might well be incidental. But the God of the Bible is nature's God, which means nature matters. It's a good through which God works because it is the work of his hands.

The God of the Bible is nature's God, which means nature matters.

I was visiting Rob Clark, a fellow pastor in Bournemouth, England. Rob took me to the seacoast not far from where the Normandy invasion was launched in World War II. He pointed to the top of a high bluff overlooking the sea and said, "Ken, if you climb up that mountain, God will speak to you when you get to the top. He does for me every time."

I chugged up the steep slope, smiling at Rob's naïveté. That was a mistake. The smiling probably got my endorphins going, as did the vigorous exercise. When I got to the top, the view was spectacular—the kind my brain rewards with a burst of happy chemicals.

This left me vulnerable. Despite my intention to prove Rob wrong, I couldn't help but stand there in a posture of receptivity, and as clear as a gentle bell at a distance, I heard in my head these surprising words: *You will live a long time.* Was it the voice of God? It felt like it to me. It spoke to a fear that I had of dying young, which hasn't bothered me since. Time, in this case, will tell if the voice was speaking the truth.

And when I walked down to the base of the bluff where Rob

was waiting for me, I could only shrug sheepishly when he greeted me with an inordinately large grin that said, "*I told you so!*"

Jesus Praying in a Pocket Park

Fortunately, in many urban settings, we've had the good sense to create little nature preserves called pocket parks. The Mount of Olives was such a place. Jesus went there often when he was in town to get away from the nightlife. At the base of the Mount of Olives was the Garden of Gethsemane. *Gethsemane* means olive press—where olives were placed under intense pressure to squeeze the oil out.

It's no accident that Jesus prayed through some intense, squeezing pressure in the Garden of Gethsemane.

Jesus and His Favorite Prayer Places

Of all the outdoor places Jesus prayed, he seemed to have a preference for the wilderness:

- "Jesus Himself would often slip away to the wilderness and pray" (Luke 5:16 NASB).
- "Immediately the Spirit impelled Him to go out into the wilderness. And He was in the wilderness forty days being tempted by Satan; and He was with the wild beasts, and the angels were ministering to Him" (Mark 1:12–13 NASB).

Wild places are important for the soul. In Howard Frumpkin's article on the health benefits of nature, he cites one researcher who has coined the term *wilderness rapture*, feelings of awe, wonder, and humility evoked by being in wild places.[10]

---

10. David Cumes, "Nature as medicine: the healing power of the wilderness," *Alternative Therapies* 1998(4): 79–86.

I wonder: is it an accident that the less contact we have with the wild, the more we think we can domesticate God?

I wouldn't know. I haven't been to many truly wild places.

My wife, Nancy, and I, two newly married city kids at the time, did a backpacking trip in the Algonquin wilderness of Northern Ontario. We didn't know what we were doing. No, really. We took canned tuna and boxes of raisins and a heavy canvas tent, cursing our ignorance as we staggered through the wilderness under a heavy load.

We didn't know about hanging your provisions from a tree to keep them away from the bears. So we got a midnight visit from an eager black bear, not knowing that black bears are not grizzly bears. We were newly reconnected-to-faith Christians at the time who hadn't worked up the nerve to pray with each other.

But the midnight visit from the black bear who might, for all we knew, have been a grizzly bear snorting around outside our tent, moved us to "call upon the name of the Lord" together for the first time. I believe my prayer went something like this: "God, please don't let us die this way!"

As I said, wild places can be good for the soul.

Prayer in a Desolate Place

Most of these outdoor praying places conveyed God's beauty. But there is one important exception: Golgotha, the place of the cross, where Jesus did his most powerful praying.

Golgotha, which means "the Place of the Skull" (Mark 15:22), was a place where the Romans executed insurrectionists. Like Gehenna, the place outside Jerusalem that served as a kind of toxic dump where the fires never went out, Golgotha couldn't have been a beautiful place.

In that God-forsaken zone, the most terrifying and the most beautiful, and perhaps the most powerful prayers ever heard were uttered:

"My God, My God, why have you forsaken me?"

"Father, forgive them, they don't know what they are doing."

"It is finished."

"Into your hands I commend my spirit."

It is as though the ugliness of our souls is expressed in the ugly places we make on this earth.

It is as though his cleansing of one is necessary for the cleansing of the other.

It is as though the whole creation longs for its liberation from decay, because it has a stake in our redemption.

The location of the outdoor praying places is not incidental.

Needing to Get Out More

Are you having a dull or a difficult time praying? Maybe you are praying too often in a dull or a difficult place. Maybe you need to get out a little more.

Scouting Around for Your Favorite Praying Places

Jesus had his favorite outdoor praying places, but you probably don't live where he did. So go hunting for your own favorite praying places. You may have found some already or have a good idea where they might be. These are places that invite you to pray by your simply being in them. They are places in which you could pray aloud without drawing attention to yourself. They are places you are eager to enter and reluctant to leave.

Find several such places while you're at it: one that is close to home, another that is within walking distance, another that is only a short drive away, and still another that you can only visit like a pilgrim going on pilgrimage.

My favorite praying places (near to far, in order) are my front porch overlooking a lawn with oak trees and my wife's extravagant flower beds; the empty bleachers at the nearby high school track surrounded by woods; a spot next to the Huron River in the Arboretum, a nature area next to the campus at the University of Michigan, and Yosemite National Park, which I've visited only once and need to get back to again, now that I think of it.

Taking a Walk

I know several who find it very difficult to pray while sitting still, but enjoy praying while walking. The rhythmic walking is relaxing and seems to help overcome distracting thoughts. Plus it's good exercise! Saul of Tarsus was traveling (probably on foot rather than horseback) to Damascus when he had a powerful vision at around noon.[11] He might have been praying the midday prayers along with his traveling companions when Jesus himself appeared to him. So be careful. Keep your eyes out for traffic and for signs of God.

The psalmist wrote, "The heavens declare the glory of God; / the skies proclaim the work of his hands. / Day after day they pour forth speech; / night after night they display knowledge. / There is no speech or language / where their voice is not heard. / Their voice goes out through all the earth, / their words to the ends of the world" (Psalm 19:1–4).

Nature tells us of nature's God in a language that can be recognized only by a prayerful awareness. Like praying in tongues, it

---

11. Acts 9:1–19, Acts 22:3–16, and Acts 26:9–18, and notice that there's no mention of Saul getting knocked off a horse.

is a different form of speech that stimulates different areas of the brain than ordinary language does.[12]

To be heard, nature asks for a little patience, like a person who stutters. You can hurry speaking, but not hearing. For that, you need to shut your mouth and *listen*. Open your eyes and observe. Take note. Be curious. Look all you like from several different angles, but don't deface the canvas.

Nature tells us of nature's God in a language that can be recognized only by a prayerful awareness.

I took a five-day silent retreat several years ago. It wasn't my idea. It was required for a class on spiritual direction that I was taking at a Jesuit retreat center.

The point of a silent retreat, I learned, is to open up your senses by changing your normal sensory routine. You don't talk for five days. You're with other people for only a brief time each day, and they are not talking either. The retreat directors confiscate your iPod, your cell phone, and your laptop, and they don't let you out to catch the last game of the Central Division playoffs at the local sports bar. You're allowed a book or two and time to use as you please as long as you're quiet.

They started us off on the retreat—most of us being terrified by the prospect of five days of silence—with a simple exercise: take a walk. For the first ten minutes of the walk, pay close attention to what you can see. For the next ten minutes, listen to the sounds around you. Then attend to the smells, then to the textures (of the wind on your face, the cold or the heat, the feel of the ground). Ten focused minutes for each of the senses.

---

12. Andrew B. Newberg, Nancy A. Wintering, Dona Morgan, Mark R. Waldman, "The measurement of regional cerebral blood flow during glossolalia: A preliminary SPECT," *Psychiatry Research: Neuroimaging* 148 (2006), 67–71.

It's a different way to take a walk, but it begins the process of opening your senses, making them more attentive than they normally are when so many things are competing for your attention that it all seems to turn to an undifferentiated and uninteresting mush.

This is a good way to take a walk in the park.

The point of listening to nature is not to squeeze out lessons that can be put into words. The point is to learn how to listen to a different language than the ones conveyed by words. Your brain is not just a word processor.

It's no accident that nature, like awe, often leaves us speechless. That's nature's way of telling us something about ourselves in relation to God.

Bringing the Outside Inside

My wife has a problem: she cannot bring herself to get rid of any of her houseplants, and because of her green thumb they don't die on her watch.

When her mother died, Nancy inherited a bird of paradise plant that hadn't bloomed for years. She nurtured that plant for about five years, and now it blooms like clockwork. Every couple of years I was drafted into helping her move the bird of paradise to a bigger planter, until we ran out of commercially available planters. So Nancy decided to break the single bird of paradise plant into five separate pots so that each of our five children could have their own. We now have five bird of paradise plants in our home, and already they are due for a planter upgrade.

I never had much interest in plants in the house, but they are growing on me, especially in the dark and long Michigan winters. I'm learning to stop and smell the bird of paradise plants.

Now I've moved one of our four indoor northern pines,

given, innocently enough, as little handheld potted things, into my office. I sit underneath the outstretched limbs of my potted pines, in front of my office window with the bird feeder attached to the outside of the glass.

During another long Michigan winter, I pop a DVD of *Sunrise Earth* into my laptop to provide a backdrop for morning prayers.[13]

It's a wonderful feature of the outdoors: a part of it can be brought indoors.

Your mystically wired brain will appreciate it.

---

13. *Sunrise Earth: American Sunrises*, Discovery Communications, 2008.

TEN

Costly: Intimacy
and the Fire of Divine Love

Fire figures prominently in the human experience of God.

Moses in the wilderness heard God speak out of a burning bush. A pillar of fire led the people of Israel by night as they fled their Egyptian captors. One like "a son of the gods" met the three young men in a fiery furnace and they didn't so much as smell of smoke. Jesus promised to set the earth ablaze. When his Spirit descended on Pentecost, what seemed to be tongues of fire separated and rested on each person present. Our God, said the author of Hebrews, is a consuming fire.[1]

Try Praying by a Fire

From the earliest times, human beings sat around a campfire to cook, to tell stories, to warm themselves, to be together, to worship, to sing, to meditate, to pray. Much communion, in other

---

1. Exodus 3:1–5; Exodus 13:21–22; Daniel 3:25; Luke 12:49; Acts 2:3; Hebrews 12:29.

words, has taken place around a fire. When was the last time you sat around a fire?

Try it sometime. Get close to a fire in a fireplace or a wood stove or fire pit. Sit down near the fire and relax. Stare at the fire, understanding that God intends to use fire as a sign that reveals something about who he is.

Look at the fire as an artist might study it in preparation for painting it. Notice the variations in color and intensity. Each fire seems to have its own signature; consider carefully what the fire before you is doing. Listen attentively to the sounds made by the fire—the crackling, the hissing, the popping. Take the fire in. Let it occupy your thoughts for a while.

Then slip into prayer for loved ones or praise of God or thanks or meditation on a text of scripture.

Fire tells us something about love, doesn't it? The God of love is a consuming fire. Burning desire. Purifying, holy, sometimes demanding, love. God is easily pleased, but not easily satisfied.[2]

The Inevitable "But"

There's always a "but," isn't there?

When it comes to prayer that seeks communion with the divine, there is a cost. There is a cost especially when the divine that is sought is revealed in Jesus, who paid a heavy price for his intimacy with the Father, a Father who made demands on him.

Jesus made demands on his disciples, to the men and women who said, "Lord, teach us to pray!" He told them, in essence, "Be willing to leave father and mother to follow me. Do as you are told. I'm setting a pattern for you to follow: pick up your cross daily if you want to follow me" (Luke 14:26–27).

---

2. Words I heard from John Wimber that struck me as true.

Perhaps this is the time for you to put down this book and pick up *The Complete Idiot's Guide to Meditation.*[3]

Jesus, Peter, and Paul Knew There Was a Cost

Jesus, Peter, and Paul had intimate encounters with God. Specific examples of these encounters are detailed in the pages of the New Testament. In each case, there was a correspondence between two things: their having had these encounters in prayer and their being summoned to do things that would offend the religious sensibilities of their time—the orthodox, faithful-to-God sensibilities of their time.

Jesus felt the closeness of Abba Father when he was praying at the time of his baptism. Shortly thereafter he began to have table fellowship—a sign of social and spiritual intimacy—with tax collectors, whores, and other sinners,[4] knowing that this would bring him into conflict with his elders.

The risen Jesus apprehended Paul at noon (one of the periods of fixed-hour prayer observed at that time). Paul was to take Christ to the Gentiles, knowing that this would bring him into conflict with his Jewish peers (Acts 22:6–21).

Peter was caught up in a vision during his noontime prayers as well. In the vision he saw a sheet bearing "unclean animals" and was told to "rise and eat" what had been forbidden by God to eat. He objected, but his objections were overruled by the vision. He was to stop calling "unclean" what God was now purifying. He was to let Gentiles into the kingdom as Gentiles,

---

3. *The Complete Idiot's Guide to Prayer* by Mark Gali and James Stuart Bell (New York: Alpha, 2004) is excellent.

4. See Greg Carey, *Sinners: Jesus and His Earliest Followers* (Waco, TX: Baylor University Press, 2009) for an understanding of the term "sinners" in the historical and social context of the Gospels.

knowing this could bring him into conflict with his faith community (Acts 10:9–48).

God was turning the prevailing understanding of holiness on its head. This shift wasn't an abandonment of holiness: it was after all, the holy God commissioning these changes. But it was an offense to the prevailing way of doing holiness.

Jesus, Paul, and Peter had a lot of explaining to do. Especially Peter and Paul, who were by this time leaders in a movement already taking shape, already producing leaders and followers, already having social norms as well as the words of Jesus to go by.

There's a lesson here for those who seek a deeper life of prayer. A deeper life of prayer exposes you to the risk that God may tell you to do something that will be costly to you. If the New Testament sheds any light on the cost, it may include your popularity.

Willing to Be Led by the Fire of Divine Love

Jesus gave his disciples many reasons for being nervous around the fire of his love. It was burning hot for people they weren't particularly interested in being close to. It was willing to burn through fences built by people who knew that when it comes to sin, you can't be too careful. Only they forgot that sin can also lead people to build fences to try to keep love in line, and love will have none of it.

Sin can also lead people to build fences to try to keep love in line, and love will have none of it.

The messy thing about love, of course, is its particularity. We don't love humanity; we love humans who come in all sorts of very particular forms—each one different from all the rest.

One morning I came out of my office after a time of prayer, took one look at my wife, Nancy, and started crying—mournful, insistent tears. Something must have happened while I was praying to do that to me. All I knew was that I was painfully aware of the meagerness of my love for my wife. I love her more than I love anyone on the planet. One might even say I'm a devoted husband who knows how to sacrifice for his wife. My wife, Nancy, is pleased with my love and tells me so. None of that was the point of this.

So what was it? Love himself wasn't satisfied, and I knew it. Love loved her more than I could even imagine. I wasn't living up to what was possible. I wasn't living up to what was required by love.

I'm not sure I made much sense as I tried to orient my wife to what was happening to me. Something in the way she looked told me she understood, though. Her comforting me, of course, only made me more acutely aware that love was right not to be satisfied.

On another occasion, I was praying for one of my adult children, a daughter who decided many years before that my path wasn't hers. You don't need the details. But as I prayed for her, I became aware of an enormous reserve of admiration that I had for my daughter—her moxie, her willingness to be honest with herself and with me. It was something I knew that I had to tell her at the right time.

Now it's happening with Charles Darwin. I'm a friend of ocean conservationist Carl Safina who told me that though he doesn't believe in God, his two heroes are Jesus of Nazareth and Charles Darwin. That got me interested in Darwin, so I read a couple of biographies.[5] and then finally worked up the nerve to tackle his seminal work, *On the Origin of Species*.[6]

---

5. David Quammen, *The Reluctant Mr. Darwin: An Intimate Portrait of Charles Darwin and the Making of His Theory of Evolution* (New York: Atlas Books, 2006), and Janet Browne, *Darwin's Origin of Species: A Biography* (New York: Grove Press, 2006).

6. Charles Darwin, *The Origin of Species By Means of Natural Selection or The Preservation of Favoured Races in the Struggle for Life* (New York: Bantam Books, 1999), originally published 1859.

My faith community has not always viewed Charles Darwin sympathetically, to put it mildly. Many in the name of God have vilified Darwin. *Demonized* would not be too strong a word. But the man I met in the pages of *On the Origin of Species* was curious, careful to give credit to others, patient with critics, respectful of Christian faith, zealous for life in all its diverse expressions—a kind, considerate human being of staggering observational genius. I know it sounds strange, but I have a deep affection for Charles Darwin. Is that allowed? I think it is.

As a pastor, you also feel a great deal of affection for your faith community. You serve, after all, as one of them. But a pastor must always be first and foremost a disciple who is willing to follow where the master leads, even if it makes your faith community nervous.

A woman recently came to me to disclose that she was born a man but had undergone extensive surgery and was now a woman. I felt uncomfortable at first, not because of the person before me, but due to the complexities and tensions surrounding issues of gender and sexuality in my faith community. Over time, I realized that wasn't good enough. I am this woman's pastor, and I felt summoned to accept her just as she is.

I know believers who are certain that people who are confused enough about their gender to go through a long and expensive process involving psychological testing, waiting periods, hormone therapy, and multiple surgical procedures to change their gender, are by definition outside the boundaries of holiness. Such people must repent and reverse the process to return to their previous gender, it is thought. Or they must live with the reversed gender but present themselves in the gender of their birth.

I would trust that discernment more if I knew that it was coming from an actual experience of loving a real person who has struggled through this process.

So what is a pastor to do? Sometimes we think we're supposed to "fix" such people even when we're not sure what ails them. I have been given a different discernment in prayer. I am to accept the person before me as she presents herself to me, knowing that this *person*, this very real human being, is beautiful in God's eyes.

Too often, Christians are perceived as people who want to change other people, rather than people who have been summoned to love other people. Too often the perception is based in reality. This is a real shame because love is the most transforming thing going. It's just that those who are doing the loving are not in charge of the changing.

This is especially important when we consider the tenderest dimensions of our humanity, not the least of which involves gender and sexuality.

Pause in the Name of Love

There are certain things that we cannot generate in prayer, and love is one of those things. But we can be attentive to the arrival of love in prayer, so that when it comes, we can welcome it.

We experience love in our bodies. The Greek work for "compassion" is *splagchna*, a word related to the English word for spleen. We feel compassion in our innards. The vagus nerve, which runs from the top of the spinal cord to the heart, liver, and digestive tract, has been called "the nerve of compassion." When stimulated, it slows the heart rate, readies the vocal cords for speech, and releases a hormone that enables trust and bonding. It's responsible for the warm, expansive feeling in the chest associated with love, compassion, and empathy.[7] In response to the suffering of others,

---

7. "Forget Survival of the Fittest: It Is Kindness That Counts," interview with Dacher Keltner by David DiSalvo in *Scientific American Mind* 20(5): September/October 2009, 18–19.

we may feel a catch in the throat or tears welling up in our eyes; our nostrils may flare when love pays a visit.

When you notice these bodily effects, even when they are subtle or gentle, pause to welcome what is going on in your body. Sometimes love comes like a shy stranger looking for a welcome.

This may happen while you are worshipping with others, singing, listening to music, reading Scripture, watching a movie, listening to someone's story. When it happens—especially in prayer—you can pause, if you like, to receive it, to welcome it, to give it more space.

Often we're unaware of love's effects on our bodies, or what Jonathan Edwards called "the holy affections."[8] Perhaps we're uncomfortable with emotion in general, or we simply haven't bothered to notice or identify these effects. Attentiveness to God and attentiveness to love's impact on our bodies are related! The old spiritual had it right: "When the Spirit moves you, Lord, you've got to move." Jesus likened the Spirit to the wind, blowing when and where it pleases. We can't make the wind blow, but we can pause to notice it when it does.

I think you will find that with a little attentiveness and the intention to welcome these effects when they come, God may use them to expand your capacity to love others "from the heart."

The Brain Is Mystically Wired to What End?

As disciples of Jesus, we are called to participate in love, pure and simple and often *hard*. Not love as we define love, but love as love is being revealed to us in Jesus.

---

8. Jonathan Edwards, *The Religious Affections* (Carlisle, PA: Banner of Truth, 1961), first opened my eyes to the importance of these bodily effects.

Christian prayer is prayer *with* ourselves—our whole selves—but not *to* ourselves. Christian prayer requires openness to intimacy with God on his terms. This is what it means to say that God is God and we are not.

To be intimate with *anyone* begins with acceptance. God accepts us sinners. We, in turn, accept God as God.

Intimacy with God sounds spiritual, but all of life is spiritual. I'm intimate with my wife, not just because I have amorous feelings toward her. I'm intimate with Nancy because I know her name and she knows my name. I'm intimate with her because we have a common checking account. We live in the same house. We share the burdens and strains of having a family and making our way through the world. My work affects her and hers affects me. You get the picture.

Intimacy means being willing to get close enough to another person that you might, from time to time, wish they were someone else. They might feel like the wrong person for you at any particular time. You argue. You have disagreements. Maybe you occasionally infuriate each other. Of course you do, because you're open to being *close*.

All of this corresponds to our intimacy with God.

The brain is mystically wired to an end, and that end is God: to perceive God, to experience God, and most of all to *participate in* God—the God who is love, properly understood.

Love makes demands on us that nothing else can make. *Forgive those who have wronged you. Lay your life down for your friends. Treat others as you would want to be treated. Love your enemies.* Who ever thought this would be easy?

Though I once wrote a book called *Decision to Love*,[9] love is so much more than a decision. We must decide to love, but we

---

9. Ken Wilson, *Decision to Love* (Ann Arbor, MI: Servant Books, 1980).

can't love by deciding. Strictly speaking, love isn't something we do. Love is something that we participate in.

While we do things to pray, prayer itself, at least of the Christian variety, is not, strictly speaking something we do. Jesus prays and we participate with him when we pray. And this participation comes at a cost—the demands of love that are not easily satisfied. As soon as we've had enough, we don't get any more.

In your praying life, you will be made aware that Love is making one of his demands on you. It will seem hard. It may seem beyond your capacity. Fear may try to hold you back. At any rate, it will require something of you. He will require something of you. This won't happen just once, but again and again at a pace that you can handle.

You may, at a certain point, decide that you've had enough. Perhaps without admitting it to yourself, even, you will pull back from love. Love will let you pull back to what feels to you like a safer distance. Maybe it is a safer distance.

But this may not satisfy you, and you may decide that you haven't had enough, after all. Will you dance with love or by yourself? Please decide to dance with love.

The Fire Is Fine

My point is simply this: God is burning with love. God is a consuming fire because love is a consuming fire. The Father, the Son, and the Holy Spirit have been in a state of all-consuming but ever-generating love for each other from before all time. This love, being love, is reaching beyond itself, to generate an ever-expanding loving and beloved community. This is what the whole thing is about.

Come on in, if you dare; the fire is fine.

You cannot hope to be touched by this without it burning in you, in some small way. The boundaries of your heart do not shrink under the influence of this love. They expand.

We all have conventional love boundaries, comfort zones of love. This is part of being human, and it has its advantages. But it's not good enough. It's not human enough.

If you are not loving beyond your comfort zone, you are not giving love any satisfaction whatsoever. Love is not having its way with you. Love is only satisfied with more love. Like Paul said when he saw a burgeoning Jesus community on the path of loving each other, "You're doing it, loving each other! Now do so more and more" (1 Thessalonians 4:9–10). He wasn't just talking about having more potlucks either. He meant they were to dive more deeply into love, embracing the challenges to love, finding ways to love when love isn't easy, or when love is opposed by powerful fears.

We're mystically wired for more love than we ever thought existed.

This, and nothing less than this, is what we're mystically wired for. We're mystically wired for more love than we ever thought existed. We're mystically wired to do more loving than we ever thought possible. We're mystically wired to stand in the middle of love's consuming fire and not so much as smell of smoke.

You Are

The only thing standing between us and excruciating bliss is the failure to appreciate God, others, and the glorious world we find ourselves in. You must believe that you—your body, your brain, your being—can appreciate all this heaven winking at us through all this earth. You must believe you are meant for this by the Wonder who stands in, over, beyond, and behind it all.

How we get there is the only question, but that there is a somewhere to get to is something to bet your life on.

What was it about Jesus of Nazareth that brought out the crowds? What was it about him that delighted those crowds when he taught? What was it about him that led the unnamed woman to run to her dowry box, pull out the jar of alabaster, and crash the all-male dinner party at Simon's estate, breaking the ointment open over his feet and bathing those same feet with her tears and wiping them with her hair?

It was the awareness—conscious, intuitive, spiritual, reasoned, or just beyond thought—that in him was life. That Jesus could lead us all into a realm where we, too, could appreciate God, others, and the glorious world we find ourselves in.

Yes, there are many reasons we pray. We pray to get through the day. We pray to vent our anger at someone who can take it. We pray to ask, to beg, to cajole, to negotiate for the things we desire or need or simply can't live without. We pray to do something when there's nothing else to be done.

But beneath all that, maybe even infusing all that, we pray so that we might live in a realm of excruciating bliss. Everything else that we yearn for is just a taste of that, a shadow, a hint: sex, friendship, art, music, beauty, childbearing, the wind in our faces, laboring, dying.

To think that we could find some way to pray that would allow us to feel this at will, is, I suppose, an inevitable hazard of our impatient and idolatrous age. But knowing that we are born for this is like knowing that we have a guest who won't leave when it's time because he knows we don't really want him to.

A Few Things Worth Believing While You're Praying

Prayer is the art of the humanly possible. You must believe that if you are going to pray. And humanity is the art of relatedness with others, including God.

Prayer is something we can learn. Jesus learned to pray, and he was like us. The first time the subject of prayer comes up in the Gospels, the disciples are asking Jesus to teach them to pray. Oh, what an encouraging thing these Gospels are! The Gospels are not loaded with instructions on prayer that we can get busy implementing—instructions that would necessarily narrow the field of potential pray-ers and constrict the landscape of prayer for the pray-ers to inhabit. But this request—"Lord, teach us to pray!"—and his honoring of it (in contrast with other requests that Jesus refused to honor) tells us what we need to know: we can learn how to pray, and Jesus can teach us.

If nothing else, I'm inviting you to believe that, despite whatever arguments you can muster to the contrary. Ignore those arguments. How far in life has that kind of thinking gotten you? What do you know when you're thinking like that? What fruit has it borne?

Not much.

On the other hand, appreciating God, others, and the world we find ourselves in is something you have tasted,

We can learn how to pray, and Jesus can teach us.

or have caught a whiff of. People don't bother reading a book like this without that happening in their lives.

Here's a crazy fact that we are summoned to wager our lives on: there really is something there to catch a whiff of. The hints really are hinting at something rather than nothing.

Acquiring a Taste for Life

About five years ago, I happened on a piece of opera that captured me like "I Want to Hold Your Hand" did in the sixth grade. (I didn't know who she was, but I knew I wanted to hold her hand.)

But this piece of music—*Songs, Op. 34/Vocalise No. 14*—I don't even know who wrote it, or if it's part of an actual opera, I've just got it on my iPod—didn't have any words, just a voice.

Bingo! I thought. *Maybe there are other songs like this I would like.* I asked a friend trained in opera if she could recommend other songs like this one. Now I have seven songs on my opera playlist and am burning through opera like there's no tomorrow.

I love to listen to these songs while I'm praying. Sometimes it feels like just listening to these particular songs is close enough to praying until the real thing comes along.

What happened to me? Life! I began to appreciate more of

life, and it was one step closer to my heart's longing for excruciating bliss. Stick with me here: I mean a *small* step.

This morning, after a lousy night's sleep, I finally staggered into the office to pray and did my usual morning prayers, but this time, with my opera playlist playing in the background, and a *Planet Earth* DVD[1] playing on my laptop screen.

Now, I had a very tame 1960s. No LSD, no serious drugs of any kind, got drunk a few times and regretted it each time. But whatever it is that people think they can find by ingesting these substances happened to me while I watched the "Shallow Oceans" episode of *Planet Earth* on my laptop with the opera playing in the background after praying the morning office of *The Divine Hours*.

Through it all, I was thinking, or perhaps praying, "Jesus, is this part of what you meant by, 'I came that you may have life and have it to the full'?" (John 10:10). It sure felt like that to me this morning.

When my praying was over, I talked to my wife on the phone for a few minutes—the same Nancy I've known for thirty-eight years—and she sounded brand-new to me.

I'm not fool enough to say that this is supposed to happen to you or that it can happen to you if I send you the playlist and you get a copy of *Planet Earth* and do the morning office of *The Divine Hours* on the first Saturday after June 1. I'm not sure how many of you would want it to happen to you. "To each his own" applies to prayer too.

I'm saying that there's so much life around us and in us and beyond us that if we can learn how to catch the slightest traces of it in the wind, we'll never be the same.

---

1. *Planet Earth*, BBC Warner, 2007.

So Much of Our Brain Available for Prayer

There is so much in our brains that is available for prayer: appreciating and sensing connections and tasting joy and recognizing beauty and feeling love, including romantic love and dutiful love and every form in between, all part of our mystical wiring. Along with the part of our brain that runs through names on a prayer list and the part of our brain that talks to God as though he were listening, the part that sings, that reads, and so on.

I think it's important for you to believe that. You have been given a brain that is capable of many kinds of praying.

And this brain of yours, this body of yours, this being of yours is not, like you are prone to think, set in stone. Though I've borrowed the wiring metaphor, it breaks down here because your brain is not hardwired. Your brain is organically connected, pulsing and throbbing with life. You are alive because everything within you, down to the smallest quanta, is moving, vibrating, resonating with its neighbor.

Your brain is ever in the process of reprogramming itself, growing new neurons, making new connections between neurons, being shaped and influenced and changing, all the time! Yours may be changing without your even trying to help it along.

The Good News of a Renewable Mind

Just think what might be possible if we were more intentional about helping the change process along? Those stodgy old things called spiritual disciplines aren't stodgy at all. They are sophisticated tools to shape the praying brain.

The apostle Paul, born in a different time and place, might have been a neuroscientist! Centuries ago, he wrote, "Do not conform any longer to the pattern of this world, but be transformed by the renewing of your mind" (Romans 12:2). Paul understood by experience and observation and revelation what cognitive scientists have been trying to tell us over the last few years: the human brain is a work in progress and we, my friends, are renewable!

Start somewhere, anywhere, but start.

Did some specific practice mentioned in these pages catch your interest and attention? (I've included an appendix with ten practices summarized for your handy reference.) Did you think, *Maybe I could do that!* Or better yet, *I could see myself doing that.*

Stop, drop, and do that. Do it for a little while—six weeks— to let your renewable brain get used to it. Trust that despite your perceived spiritual dullness, the Creator is more powerful than the creature, and he's arranged for you, in your body, to gain a growing sense of him.

Stop focusing on what a lousy student you are in the school of prayer and start focusing on what a great teacher Jesus might be.

For once in your life, don't try to make prayer more difficult than it is. Trust that seeking to live your life with God is filled with challenges enough that you don't have to pile on ones of your own making.

Stop focusing on what a lousy student you are in the school of prayer and start focusing on what a great teacher Jesus might be.

You must believe that you—your body, your brain, your being—can appreciate all this heaven winking at us through all this earth. You must believe you are meant for this by the Wonder who stands in, over, beyond, and behind it all.

Don't give in to, don't nurse, don't make friends with the thought that you, among all people, are not made for this.

You are.

"When Jacob awoke from his sleep, he thought, 'Surely the Lord is in this place, and I was not aware of it.' He was afraid and said, 'How awesome is this place! This is none other than the house of God; this is the gate of heaven."

—GENESIS 28:16-17

Ten Practices to Explore New Realms in Prayer

The spiritual disciplines are practices that have been field-tested by people eager to connect with God over the millennia. These practices endure because they fit the way humans work. In particular, they fit the way the human brain works. There's enough variety among us that not every practice fits every person, but *some* practice fits all of us. The following ten practices, among others, are featured in *Mystically Wired* and are briefly summarized here.

1. Make a Praying Place [p. 62]

Create a spot where you live and set it aside for prayer. Make it an appealing and comfortable place that can be relatively free of distractions. The space should say something about your understanding of God and your aspirations to meet him. The existence of such a space in your living quarters will serve as a reminder that prayer isn't just something that we do; it's also a place where we go.

2. Hold Loved Ones in Memory Before Love [p. 77]

Call to mind those you love (beginning with the people you feel most connected to and have the least conflict with). Simply name each person, one at a time, and hold the loved one in memory for a moment or two (or for an extended period) before God, who is Love. During this time, don't focus on their faults, or even their pressing needs. Focus on your connection to them and their beloved place before God.

3. Adore God Through Focused Attention [p. 96]

To help calm busy thoughts that might come between you and the simple awareness of God's presence, focus your mind on something concrete and particular that is connected, in some way, to God. It may be a term of endearment for God, or some work of his hands like the burning flame of a candle or a scene of natural beauty. As your thoughts wander, which they will, renew your intention to make yourself present to God by gently returning your attention to this focal point.

4. Meditate on a Small Portion of Scripture [p. 102]

Select a small portion of Scripture (no longer than Psalm 23) and read it over slowly three times. While you are reading the text, pay attention to a verse, phrase, or image that your heart is drawn to. Return to that verse, phrase, or image to ponder it more closely. Place yourself in the text as a participant and allow the text to speak to you. Listen for the voice as well as the words of the text. Stay with it as long as you like (a minute or two is fine for starters) before moving on to a second or third verse, phrase, or image.

5. Try The Divine Hours [p. 120]

Get a copy of *The Divine Hours: A Manual for Prayer* by Phyllis Tickle (or another form of prayer at intervals through the day). After you become familiar with how it is organized, set aside a day or two to do all four prayer intervals, just to see how it works. Then begin to build it into your daily routine, starting with the interval that is easiest to remember (usually, just before bed.) Once that pattern is set, add other intervals as desired. It may take four to six weeks to add each interval into your daily pattern. Be patient with yourself and God. Don't evaluate *anything* until you've tried it for about six weeks (roughly the time frame of Lent, a great season to start).

6. Be Still and Know That I Am God Meditation [p. 134]

Meditate on this verse (Psalm 46:10) as though memorizing it, saying *Be* . . . , then Be *still* . . . , then Be still *and* . . . , then Be still and *know* . . . , until you have completed the verse using this pattern. Take your time, a full relaxing breath in and out for each segment. No extra credit for speed. Place special emphasis or focus on the newly introduced word (indicated by italics here) as you say it aloud or silently.

7. Breathe the Jesus Prayer [p. 141]

Link the phrasing of the Jesus Prayer ("Lord Jesus Christ, Son of the living God, have mercy on me, a sinner"—or simplified variations) to your breathing. For example, pray, "Lord Jesus Christ, Son of the living God" as you inhale and "have mercy on me, a sinner" as you exhale. Breathe in a relaxed and peaceful manner. Take a few minutes at first to establish the rhythm of the prayer tied to your breathing, then continue to focus on the words of the prayer as you breathe in and out, for a specified period of time (say, five to ten minutes). As your thoughts wander, gently return your focus to the words of the prayer.

8. Find a Favorite Spot in the Outdoor Cathedral [p. 161]

Look for a place outdoors that reminds you of the beauty, goodness, and glory of life and of God. Pay special attention to places that seem to invite you to linger. Go there with the intention of enjoying God's creation as a way to signal your appreciation for being alive. If possible, identify three such places: near your home, within easy walking or driving distance, and for rare visits.

9. Take a Prayer Walk [p. 162]

Find a relaxing place to walk. Once you've settled into a sustainable stride and know what route you're on, slip into prayer of whatever kind: thanksgiving, prayer for loved ones (walking works particularly well with practice 2) or reflecting on memorized portions of Scripture or hymns.

10. Pray with Your Eyes Open by the Fire [p. 167]

Sit near a fireplace, fire pit, campfire, or in a pinch, near a lit candle. As you pray (in whatever manner you have chosen) keep your eyes open and focused on the fire. Notice the sights, sounds, and smells associated with the fire. Move between focusing on the fire and focusing on your prayers, or focus on both simultaneously as we do when speaking to people in person.

About the Author

Ken Wilson is the senior pastor of Vineyard Church of Ann Arbor and a member of the national board of Vineyard, A Community of Churches. Ken is the coauthor (with Rich Nathan) of *Empowered Evangelicals: Bringing Together the Best of the Evangelical and Charismatic Worlds* (Ampelon, 1995) and the author of *Jesus Brand Spirituality: He Wants His Religion Back* (Thomas Nelson, 2008).

Ken is active in the effort to restore environmental stewardship to the American Christian community as an integral component of discipleship. He is a participant with Evangelicals and Scientists United to Protect Creation, a cooperative effort of environmental scientists and evangelical faith leaders to bridge the cultural divide that has done so much to keep people of faith from exercising their duty to God and his creation. Ken founded Creation Care for Pastors (www.creationcareforpastors.com) to educate evangelical pastors regarding the global environmental crisis. With ocean conservationist Carl Safina, he is the cofounder of the Friendship Collaborative (www.friendshipcollaborative. org), which brings together secular environmental scientists and faith leaders on university campuses to explore their common concern for the environment.

Ken and his wife, Nancy, live in Ann Arbor, Michigan. They have five children and five grandchildren.

Visit his blog, kenwilsononline.com.